grammar
and
word study

Book C

CW00495668

CURRICULUM

- Parts of speech
- Understanding and choosing words
- Punctuation
- Figures of speech

Primary grammar and word study *(Book C)*

Published by Prim-Ed Publishing 2010
Reprinted Prim-Ed Publishing 2014
Copyright© by R.I.C. Publications® 2008
ISBN 978-1-84654-207-7
PR–6242

Titles available in this series:

Primary grammar and word study *(Book A)*
Primary grammar and word study *(Book B)*
Primary grammar and word study *(Book C)*
Primary grammar and word study *(Book D)*
Primary grammar and word study *(Book E)*
Primary grammar and word study *(Book F)*
Primary grammar and word study *(Book G)*

Internet websites

In some cases, websites or specific URLs may be recommended. While these are checked and rechecked at the time of publication, the publisher has no control over any subsequent changes which may be made to webpages. It is *strongly* recommended that the class teacher checks *all* URLs before allowing pupils to access them.

View all pages online   **Website:** www.prim-ed.com

Primary grammar and word study – Book C
Foreword

Primary grammar and word study is a series of seven books designed to introduce pupils to parts of speech, ways to understand and choose words, punctuation and figures of speech.

Titles in this series:

- *Primary grammar and word study Book A* (Ages 5–6)
- *Primary grammar and word study Book B* (Ages 6–7)
- *Primary grammar and word study Book C* (Ages 7–8)
- *Primary grammar and word study Book D* (Ages 8–9)
- *Primary grammar and word study Book E* (Ages 9–10)
- *Primary grammar and word study Book F* (Ages 10–11)
- *Primary grammar and word study Book G* (Ages 11–12)

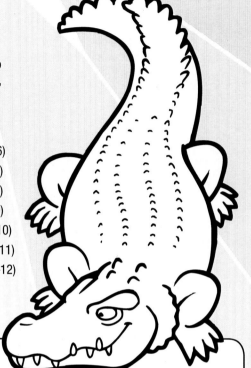

Contents

Teachers notes

Learning about grammar and studying words helps pupils to better comprehend and use language when they are reading, writing, speaking, listening and viewing. Pupils can use the 'rules' or features of grammar to make their own writing and speaking understood by others and to understand the writing and speaking of others.

One major reference used during the writing of this series was the work of Professor George Stern, who was a member of the Systemic Functional Grammar Association and PEN International.

Functional grammarians consider the way in which words are used within the context of a sentence; that is, they are more concerned with their FUNCTION in a particular context. In traditional grammar, the focus is more on defining the different parts of speech.

The book has been organised into four main sections, covering a variety of aspects of grammar and word study:

• Parts of speech   • Understanding and choosing words   • Punctuation   • Figures of speech

Groups of two pages within each section follow a similar format.

Each pupil page is accompanied by a corresponding teachers page.

> Prim-Ed Publishing® follows the guidelines for punctuation and grammar as recommended by the
> *Style manual for authors, editors and printers, sixth edition, 2002.*
> Note, however, that teachers should use their own guide if there is a conflict.

Teachers notes pages

The **focus** of each corresponding pupil page is given.

A **definition** of each focus is given. For younger pupils, the definitions may be written in a more 'child-friendly' manner on the pupil page. For older pupils, the definition will be the same as that on the teachers page.

One or two **examples** of the focus are also given.

An **explanation** is given of the focus. This may also include the purpose for learning about the focus.

Any necessary information about how to use the worksheet with the pupils is also provided.

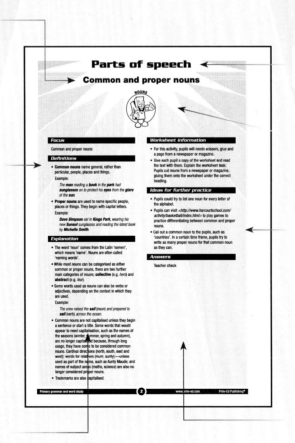

The **title** of each section is given.

A **literacy character** for each focus provides a visual identification of each focus on the pupils page.

Ideas for further practice to support or extend the pupil activity on the worksheet are supplied. Where possible, the activities will include other key learning areas or other areas of English, such as speaking and listening.

Answers are provided for pupil pages where necessary.

Teachers notes

The **focus** of each pupil page is given. For younger pupils, the focus may be written in a more 'child-friendly' manner.

A **literacy character** for each focus provides a visual identification of each focus on the pupil page. Further information about the literacy characters can be found on pages vi and vii.

The **focus** is used **in context** in an appropriate text. A variety of different texts have been used on pupil pages.

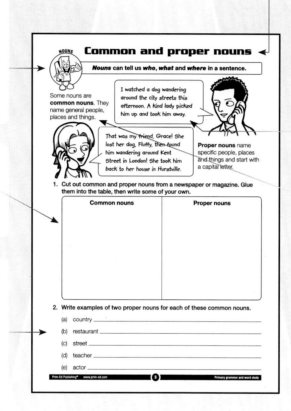

A **definition of the focus** is given, which may be written in a more 'child-friendly' manner for younger pupils. For older pupils, the definition will be the same as that on the teachers page.

Interesting activities expect the pupils to **use and practise the focus** or to create examples of his/her own.

Clear, concise **instructions** for completing the pupil activities are supplied.

Activities on the pupil page require the pupils to **identify the focus** in context to see how and why it is used.

Note:

The pupil page activities give only a brief introduction to some of the concepts of grammar and word study included in this series of books. It is expected that teachers will use other resources and provide other activities to consolidate and extend pupils' understanding of these concepts and to introduce other age-appropriate grammar and word study concepts.

Teachers notes

Literacy characters appear on each pupil page throughout the series. The 'fun' characters provide a representation which is easily recognisable for visual-spatial learners and teachers to facilitate learning and teaching. Teachers may use the characters to select appropriate pupil pages throughout the different books in the series for individual pupil learning.

Parts of speech

NOUNS

VERBS

ADJECTIVES

ADVERBS

CONJUNCTIONS

PRONOUNS

DETERMINERS

PREPOSITIONS

Understanding and choosing words

HOMOGRAPHS

HOMOPHONES

WORD GROUPS

PLURALS

SYNONYMS

ANTONYMS

CONFUSED WORDS

Teachers notes

Literacy characters appear on each pupil page throughout the series. The 'fun' characters provide a representation which is easily recognisable for visual-spatial learners and teachers to facilitate learning and teaching. Teachers may use the characters to select appropriate pupil pages throughout the different books in the series for individual pupil learning.

Punctuation

Figures of speech

Parts of speech checklist

Name of pupil	Nouns	Verbs	Adjectives	Adverbs	Pronouns	Conjunctions	Determiners	Prepositions

Understanding and choosing words checklist

Name of pupil	Homographs	Homophones	Word groups	Plurals	Synonyms	Antonyms	Confused words

Punctuation checklist

Name of pupil	Full stops	Question marks	Exclamation marks	Capital letters	Commas	Apostrophes	Quotation marks
			X				

Figures of speech checklist

Name of pupil	Alliteration	Anagrams/ Palindromes	Metaphors	Similes	Onomatopoeia	Personification

Curriculum links

Country	Subject	Level	Objectives
England	English	Year 3	• spell further homophones • spell words that are often misspelt • extend the range of sentence with more than one clause by using a wider range of conjunctions • choose nouns or pronouns appropriately for clarity and cohesion and to avoid repetition • use conjunctions, adverbs and prepositions to express time and cause • indicate possession by using the possessive apostrophe with singular and plural nouns • use and punctuate direct speech • use of the forms *a* or *an* according to whether the next word begins with a consonant or a vowel • word families based on common words, showing how words are related in form and meaning • use of the present perfect form of verbs instead of the simple past
Northern Ireland	Language and Literacy	Key Stage 1	• recognise features of spoken language, showing phonological awareness; e.g. rhyming words • build up a sight vocabulary • recognise how words are constructed and spelt • understand and use a range of vocabulary by investigating and experimenting with language • spell correctly a range of familiar, important and regularly occurring words • develop increasing confidence in the use of grammar and punctuation
Republic of Ireland	English Language	2nd Class	• experience challenging vocabulary • build a sight vocabulary of common words • engage in activities designed to increase awareness of sounds • learn about the sounds associated with the part of a word or syllable that allows it to rhyme with another word or syllable • experiment with more elaborate vocabulary • understand that the conventions of punctuation help to make meaning clearer in writing • spell correctly a range of words • perform alphabetical order tasks
Scotland	Literacy and English	First	• explore word patterns • use knowledge of sight vocabulary, punctuation and grammar • spell commonly used words and use knowledge of letter patterns and spelling rules • use appropriate punctuation • order sentences in a way that makes sense
Wales	English	Key Stage 2	• use a range of sentence structures and vocabulary with precision • engage in activities that focus on words • use punctuation to clarify meaning, including full stop, exclamation and question marks, comma, apostrophe and speech marks • choose and use appropriate vocabulary • use nouns, pronouns, adjectives, adverbs, prepositions, connectives and verb tenses

Notes

Parts of speech

Common and proper nouns

Focus

Common and proper nouns

Definitions

- **Common nouns** name general, rather than particular, people, places and things.

  Example:

  *The **man** reading a **book** in the **park** had **sunglasses** on to protect his **eyes** from the **glare** of the **sun**.*

- **Proper nouns** are used to name specific people, places or things. They begin with capital letters.

  Example:

  ***Dave Simpson** sat in **Kings Park**, wearing his new **Sunsol** sunglasses and reading the latest book by **Michelle Smith**.*

Explanation

- The word 'noun' comes from the Latin 'nomen', which means 'name'. Nouns are often called 'naming words'.

- While most nouns can be categorised as either common or proper nouns, there are two further main categories of nouns; **collective** (e.g. *herd*) and **abstract** (e.g. *fear*).

- Some words used as nouns can also be verbs or adjectives, depending on the context in which they are used.

  Example:

  *The crew raised the **sail** (noun) and prepared to **sail** (verb) across the ocean.*

- Common nouns are not capitalised unless they begin a sentence or start a title. Some words that would appear to need capitalisation, such as the names of the seasons (winter, summer, spring and autumn), are no longer capitalised because, through long usage, they have come to be considered common nouns. Cardinal directions (north, south, east and west); words for relatives (mum, aunty);—unless used as part of the name, such as Aunty Maude; and names of subject areas (maths, science) are also no longer considered proper nouns.

- Trademarks are also capitalised.

Worksheet information

- For this activity, pupils will needs scissors, glue and a page from a newspaper or magazine.

- Give each pupil a copy of the worksheet and read the text with them. Explain the worksheet task: Pupils cut nouns from a newspaper or magazine, gluing them onto the worksheet under the correct heading.

Ideas for further practice

- Pupils could try to list one noun for every letter of the alphabet.

- Pupils can visit *<http://www.harcourtschool.com/activity/basketball/index.html>* to play games to practice differentiating between common and proper nouns.

- Call out a common noun to the pupils, such as 'countries'. In a certain time frame, pupils try to write as many proper nouns for that common noun as they can.

Answers

Teacher check

Common and proper nouns

| Nouns can tell us who, what and where in a sentence. |

Some nouns are **common nouns**. They name general people, places and things.

I watched a dog wandering around the city streets this afternoon. A kind lady picked him up and took him away.

That was my friend, Grace! She lost her dog, Fluffy, then found him wandering around Kent Street in London! She took him back to her house in Hurstville.

Proper nouns name specific people, places and things and start with a capital letter.

1. Cut out common and proper nouns from a newspaper or magazine. Glue them into the table, then write some of your own.

Common nouns	Proper nouns

2. Write examples of two proper nouns for each of these common nouns.

   (a) country _____

   (b) restaurant _____

   (c) street _____

   (d) teacher _____

   (e) actor _____

Parts of speech

Collective nouns

Focus

Collective nouns

Definition

- **Collective nouns** are used to name groups of people, animals and things.

  Example:

  crowd, pack, class, bunch

Explanation

- A collective noun represents a group made up of more than one person or thing; for example, a *committee*, *team*, or *family* cannot consist of one member—at least two people must compose the unit.

- A collective noun can be considered singular or plural. When referring to the collective group, the singular tends to be used when all members of the collective noun are doing the same thing at the same time.

  Example:

  *The team **is** flying to Melbourne for the finals.*

  However, when referring to the individual members of the team, the plural can be used.

  Example:

  *The team **are** going **their** separate ways.*

- 'Terms of venery' are collective nouns for types of animals, such as a **murder** of crows and a **parliament** of rooks. Sometimes a **term of venery** will apply to a group only in a certain context; for example, a *'paddling of ducks'* only refers to ducks on water.

- Learning collective nouns increases pupils' vocabulary and provides a way to categorise things with common elements.

Worksheet information

- Give each pupil a copy of the worksheet and read the poem with them. Discuss how sometimes when there is a group of things that are similar or the same, we call that group a special name. Calling groups a special name helps makes speech quicker and more accurate. Read the examples of collective nouns and ask pupils to make suggestions as to other collective nouns they know.

For example; a group of people teaching at a school are called *'staff'*.

- Pupils complete the worksheet by naming the three groups represented by the pictures, writing the collective nouns for the animal groups from the words provided, and creating their own collective nouns for the groups suggested. They can use their made-up words in a poem or story.

Ideas for further practice

- Pupils can practise identifying collective nouns at *<http://www.learnenglish.org.uk/CET/flashactivities/collective_nouns.html>*, and play concentration-style games, matching common and collective nouns, at *<http://www.quia.com/cc/150566.html>*.

- Sit pupils in a circle, with another standing in the middle. Give each pupil sitting one of five animal names.

  Example:

  wolf, cow, fish, dolphin, kitten

  The pupil in the middle calls out the collective noun for one of these groups.

  Example:

  pod, pack, school, herd, litter

  All pupils who were given the name of the animal that forms that collective noun must stand up and swap places with another pupil who has that same animal name. The person in the middle tries to take one of the free spaces. The pupil who doesn't get a space becomes the person in the middle and calls out the next collective noun.

- Make a set of paired animal collective noun cards; for example, write *pod, pack, litter, swarm* on two cards each.

  Each pupil receives a card that is one of a pair. Pupils must find their partner only by making the sound of the animal that belongs to that collective noun.

Answers

1. (a) pod   (b) pack/deck/hand
   (c) team

2. (a) school   (b) pod   (c) swarm
   (d) litter   (e) pack   (f) herd

3. Teacher check

Collective nouns

If you drove past some fluffy sheep,
Would you mention them one-by-one?
Say to your friend, 'Quick, take a peek.
There's one sheep and one sheep, plus one.
And more plus some, then another eight,
Standing together near that rock!'
Or would it be quicker to say,
'Hey, take a look at that big flock!'?

NOUNS

A ***collective noun*** is the name for a group of animals, people or things.

A **gaggle** is a group of geese.
A **library** is a group of books.
A **class** is a group of pupils.

1. **Name these groups.**

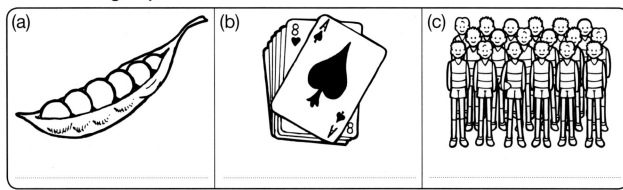

(a) ....

(b) ....

(c) ....

2. **Match the collective nouns to each group of animals.**

pod   school   litter   swarm   pack   herd

(a) fish   _____   (b) whales   _____

(c) bees   _____   (d) puppies   _____

(e) wolves   _____   (f) cows   _____

3. (a) Make up your own collective noun for one of the following groups.

   boys   shells   girls   smelly shoes

   (b) Write a poem or story about your collective noun on back of this sheet.

Parts of speech

Verbs

Focus

Finite verbs, the verbs 'to be' and 'to have'

Definition

- **Verbs** are words which show actions or states of being or having.

  Example:

    *The boy **plays** football.*
    *The new girl **is** shy.*
    *We **have** new neighbours.*

  The verb 'plays' tells about an action, 'is' tells about the state of being and 'have' tells about the state of having.

Explanation

- Verbs must have someone 'doing' the action. This is the subject of the sentence.

  In the examples above, the actions are done by 'the boy', ' the new girl ' and 'we'.

- The verbs 'to be' and 'to have' have many forms which change with the subject and the tense—see the chart below.

Person	Pronoun	The verb 'to be' Present	Past	the verb 'to have' Present	Past
First	I	am	was	have	had
Second	you	are	were	have	had
Third	he/she/it	is	was	has	had
First	we	are	were	have	had
Second	you	are	were	have	had
Third	they	are	were	have	had

Note: The future tense of the verb 'to be' is *will be* and 'to have' is *will have*.

- Every sentence must contain a verb.
- Some verbs have more than one part.

  Example:

    *He **has eaten** dinner.* (**has** is an auxiliary verb)

- Verbs can be finite or non-finite. Finite verbs change in form to match their subject or to indicate tense.

  Example:

    go → goes → went

Non-finite verbs do not change. They include:

present participles
Example: *parking*

past participles
Example: *parked*

infinitives
Example: *to park*

Worksheet information

- Read the limerick with the class, emphasising the verbs, especially those with two parts. Pupils then underline other verbs.

- Read and discuss the Question 2 sentences with the pupils. The concept of 'being' or 'having' can be difficult at this stage. The previous chart may assist understanding and identification.

- Ask the pupils to read the sentences in Question 3 to themselves and insert a suitable single verb. Ensure that the sentences sound 'right' when read quietly.

Ideas for further practice

- Involve the class in songs and fun dances—such as the macarena or the song 'Agadoo'—which involve actions.

- Play 'Pass the sentence'. Think of a short sentence with a simple verb showing action.

  Example:

    Jason struck the ball.

In groups of six, each pupil adds one action to the previous one to create a short story. The last person in the group must remember all the actions added by each person.

  Example:

    Jason struck the ball, dropped the bat, touched first base, slid over second base, jumped over third base and barrelled into the coach.

- Write examples of verbs, including ones with two parts, on slips of paper and drop them into a box or large container. Pupils must dip for a verb and use it orally or written in a sentence.

Answers

1. was, rose, reached, hid

2. (a) moved, drove
   (b) is, will be
   (c) had, have

4. (a) were   (b) had
   (c) be   (d) am

Verbs

Verbs are words which can show action, or tell about being or having.

1. Read the limerick and underline the verbs. There are some which have more than one word. They are underlined.

There once was a baker from Gid

Who <u>forgot to put</u> on the lid.

The stew rose so high

It reached to the sky.

The birds <u>were</u> so <u>scared</u> that they hid!

2. Read the sentences and underline the verbs.

- Yesterday, we moved to our new house.

- It is very exciting.

- We had lots of suitcases in our car.

- Dad drove all the way.

- We will be at out new home soon.

- My brother and I always have fun in the car.

(a) Which verbs show action? _____

(b) Which verbs show being? _____

(c) Which verbs show having? _____

3. Complete the sentences by using the correct form of the verb 'to be' or the verb 'to have'.

(a) When we left our old house and friends, all the members of my

family _____ sad.

(b) Deefer, our dog, was sad because he _____ to travel in the back of the car with the suitcases.

(c) I will _____ very glad when we finally get to our new house.

(d) I hope that I _____ going to make new friends quickly.

Parts of speech

Verbs

Focus

Command verbs (imperatives)

Definition

- **Command verbs** are used to order, command or instruct.
  Example:
  > **Close** the door!
  > **Feed** the cat!
  > **Do** your homework!

Explanation

- Verbs can describe actions ('doing' words) and must have someone 'doing' the action. Refer to pages 6 and 7 for revision.
- Most verbs describe actions but verbs also show states of 'being' or 'having'. These include the verbs 'is', 'has', 'are', 'am', 'have', 'had' and 'was'.
- Every sentence must contain a verb.
- Command verbs are commonly used when writing procedures or instructions and are often the first word in the sentence.

Worksheet information

- Pupils read the modified procedure independently with minimal assistance.
- Pupils identify the command verb at the beginning of each line, circling it. They then read the definition for command verbs.
- Explain the definition and give other examples to the pupils. Ask the pupils to supply examples as well; for example, orders from Mum or Dad at home.
- Single command verbs should be used to complete the sentences in Question 3.
- Before pupils write the instructions for tying shoelaces, revise the steps used to tie shoelaces and give examples of one or two sentences of the instructions using command verbs.
- Conclude the activity by asking pupils to give their instructions orally to a classmate after teacher checking.

Ideas for further practice

- Play games such as 'Simon says' where pupils must follow commands or orders.
- Write a favourite recipe as a class using command verbs.
- Identify command verbs in books during shared reading times.

Answers

1. Teacher check

2. Collect, Pour, Add, Add, Mix

3. Answers may vary but may include:
   (a) Tie
   (b) Stop
   (c) dig
   (d) Put/Place

4.–5. Teacher check

Command verbs

1. Read the procedure for making goo.

   - Collect all the materials—a 500 g box of cornstarch, $1\frac{1}{2}$ cups water, food colouring, a bowl.
   - Pour the cornstarch into the bowl.
   - Add the water.
   - Add about 15 drops of food colouring.
   - Mix the goo using your hands.

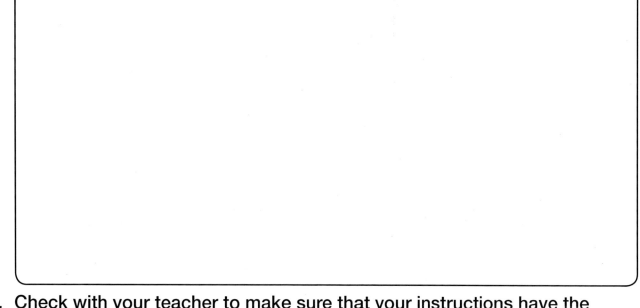

2. Circle the words at the beginning of each sentence. These five words are all command verbs.

A **command verb** is a word used to order, command or instruct.

---

3. Write a command verb to complete each sentence.

   VERBS

   (a) '_____ your shoelaces', said Mum.

   (b) '_____ that!' yelled Dad. 'You'll hurt yourself.'

   (c) 'Don't _____ holes in the garden!' said Barry to the cat.

   (d) '_____ your finished work on that pile!' said the teacher.

4. In the box below, write instructions for tying your shoelaces. Begin each instruction with a command verb.

5. Check with your teacher to make sure that your instructions have the correct verbs, then say them to a classmate for him or her to follow.

Parts of speech

Verbs

Focus

Past, present and future tense (including irregular verbs); auxiliary verbs

Definitions

- **Verb tense** shows whether the action of the verb occurs in the present, the past or the future.
- **Auxiliary verbs** are small verbs, often a form of the verb 'to be' or 'to have', that combine with another verb to form a compound verb.

  Example:

  *He **was** running.*

  *We **have** tried hard.*

Explanation

- Most verbs describe actions but verbs also show states of 'being' or 'having'.

  Example:

  *Bianca **is** sad.*

  *We **have** a new car.*

- There are three basic verb tenses—past, present and future. These tenses are often formed using an auxiliary or helping verb such as 'is', 'can', 'had' and 'will'.

  Example:

  *I **jump**. Bill **jumps**. Ken is **jumping**.*
  (present tense)

  *David **jumped**. He has **jumped**.*
  (past tense)

  *Fred will **jump**.*
  (future tense)

- Some verb tense forms are regular but many are irregular.

  Example:

  *I **buy** lunch on Mondays. (present tense)*

  *I **bought** my lunch yesterday. (past tense)*

Worksheet information

- Remind the pupils about the function of a verb. Read the explanation and text with the pupils and discuss. Ensure that the pupils realise that some verbs have two parts, such as 'were worried' and 'will catch'.
- Ask pupils to orally give examples of sentences

which include past, present and future tense verbs. Write some on the board and highlight the auxiliary verbs.

- Explain that there is more than one correct answer before pupils complete Questions 4 independently.
- Explain to the pupils that some verbs change completely rather than add auxiliary verbs (parts) to make a different tense. These verbs are called irregular verbs. Give some examples. (A list of common irregular verbs can be accessed on the Internet.) Pupils can complete the table in Question 5.

Ideas for further practice

- Both orally and in written form, change sentences from present to past or future tense or from past to future tense.
- List and display common auxiliary words which can be used to show present, past or future tense, such as 'am', 'was' and 'will'.

Answers

1. swarm, cluster, speed, scuttle, bump, flashes

2. (a) beeped, hurried, were worried, had slept, looked
   (b) were worried, had slept

3. will be, will flutter, will catch, will rest

4. Answers include:
   (a) has/had/have   (b) is/was/were/are
   (c) has/had/have   (d) will
   (e) is/was/were/are
   (f) is/has/had/was/have/were/are

5.

Present	Past	Future
(a) catch	caught	will catch
(b) see	saw	will see
(c) ride	rode	will ride
(d) go	went	will go

Present, past and future verbs

Verbs can tell about what is happening now (in the present).

1. Underline the present tense verbs.

   Pedestrians swarm like bees and cluster on the footpath. Cars, buses and bikes speed past. Feet scuttle and bags bump as soon as the green light flashes.

   Verbs can tell about what happened in the past.

2. (a) Underline the past tense verbs.

   Car horns beeped as impatient workers hurried across the street. Some were worried because they had slept in. They looked unhappy.

   (b) Which verbs have two parts? _____ and _____

   Verbs can tell about what will happen in the future.

3. Underline the future tense verbs.

   I will be a soft, white butterfly. I will flutter above heads, snarling traffic and smokey air. Then, I will catch a passing breeze up to a leafy branch, where I will rest my wings.

4. Choose words in the box to add to those below so each verb has two parts.

will	is	has	had	was	have	were	are

   (a) _____ walked   (b) _____ looking

   (c) _____ been   (d) _____ rain

   (e) _____ going   (f) _____ carried

5. Complete the table to show how these 'irregular' verbs change.

	Present	Past	Future
(a)	catch	caught	will catch
(b)		saw	
(c)	ride		
(d)	go		

Parts of speech
Adjectives

Focus

Common adjectives

Definition

- An **adjective** is a describing word. It adds meaning to or changes the meaning of a noun or a pronoun.
  Example:

  *These are **comfortable** shoes.*
  (describes the noun, 'shoes')

  *The car is **shiny**.*
  (describes the noun, 'car')

  Note: The adjective does not always come before the noun.

  *She is **kind**.*
  (describes the pronoun, 'she')

Explanation

The use of suitable adjectives not only makes our written or spoken language more interesting, it gives the reader or listener a clearer understanding.

Worksheet information

- Discuss what a describing word or adjective is with the pupils. Ask them to think of a suitable word to describe the colour/type of their eyes, hair or an article of clothing they are wearing.
  Example:

  *I have **brown** eyes.*

  *I have **straight** hair.*

  *I'm wearing **white** socks.*

  Encourage them to use the adjective in context in a sentence.
- Read the story 'A visit from Planet Pogo' with the pupils, helping them to identify the adjectives. If pupils first identify the noun, they can ask questions such as 'What kind?' in front of it to find the adjective; for example, in the first sentence, the word 'noise' is a noun in this context.

Ask: 'What kind of noise?' and the answer is 'A loud noise' (i.e. 'loud' is the adjective). Point out that not all nouns will have a word that describes them; e.g. 'homework' in line 1. Note: The first word in sentence 4, 'It', is a pronoun representing the noun 'spaceship' and the adjective that describes it is 'silver'.

- Pupils answer the questions, highlighting or circling the adjectives in the story. This activity is intended to reinforce the importance of choosing suitable adjectives to make a story more interesting and to give the reader/listener a clearer picture.
- In Activity 2, pupils can choose more than one adjective to describe their alien. Share pupil responses with the class when the activities are completed.

Ideas for further practice

- Give pairs of pupils a paper bag (or similar) with an object inside. Pupils decide on four suitable adjectives to describe the object and write them in large letters on a sheet of paper. They hold up the words and other pupils try to guess what is in the bag. Further adjectives can be suggested if pupils are unable to guess.
- Display an object from the classroom or a large picture that represents a noun such as a building or an animal. Pupils brainstorm to list suitable adjectives to describe it. Suggest more inappropriate examples and ask pupils why they are not suitable.
  Example:

  'skinny' would not describe an apple.

Answers

1. (a) a **loud** noise
   (b) **silver**
   (c) a **dust** storm
   (d) a **large** bucket, **old** cloths and the **green garden** hose
   (e) a **shiny, silver** spaceship

2.–3. Teacher check

Adjectives – 1

> *Adjectives* are describing words.

The story below has adjectives that help to make it more interesting and clearer for the reader. Read the story and answer the questions below to help you find some of the adjectives.

A visit from Planet Pogo

As my brother and I were doing our homework, we heard a loud noise. We rushed outside and couldn't believe our eyes. A spaceship had landed! It was silver and it had black blobs all over it. As we walked towards it, a door opened and an alien stepped out.

'Greetings Earthlings', the alien said. 'My name is Zogo. I am from the planet Pogo. I have dropped in to wash my dirty spaceship. It went through a dust storm and came out with black blobs all over it.'

'Hi Zogo', I replied. 'I'm Dane and this is Matt. We'll help you to wash it.'

I fetched a large bucket, old cloths and the green garden hose. In no time, Zogo had a shiny, silver spaceship. After thanking us, he soon zoomed off into outer space.

---

1. **As you answer the questions, highlight the adjectives used.**

    (a) What kind of noise did the boys hear? a _____ noise

    (b) What colour was the spaceship when it first arrived? _____

    (c) What made it dirty? a _____ storm

    (d) What did they use to clean it? a _____ bucket, _____

    cloths and the _____ _____ hose

    (e) What did it look like afterwards? a _____, _____ spaceship.

2. **Write adjectives next to the body parts to describe what you think the alien might have looked like.**

    (a) _____ eyes   (b) _____ hair

    (c) _____ arms   (d) _____ ears

    (e) _____ legs   (f) _____ body

3. **Draw your alien on the back of this sheet.**

Parts of speech
Adjectives

Focus

Common adjectives

Definition

- An **adjective** is a describing word. It adds meaning to or changes the meaning of a noun or a pronoun.

    Example:

    These are **scruffy** shoes.
    (describes the noun, 'shoes')

    The car is **fast**.
    (describes the noun, 'car')

    Note: The adjective does not always come before the noun.

    She is **beautiful**.
    (describes the pronoun, 'she')

Explanation

The use of suitable adjectives not only makes written or spoken language more interesting, it gives the reader or listener a clearer understanding.

Worksheet information

- Revise adjectives. (Use the information on page 12.)
- Discuss the importance of choosing the correct adjectives so the person listening or reading gets a clear and accurate picture. Have an object hidden from the pupils' view (e.g. a tennis ball) and tell them some words that are adjectives to describe the ball (such as 'small', 'round', 'bouncy' and 'pale green'). Pupils try to guess the object.
- The activities on page 15 are intended to reinforce the importance of choosing suitable adjectives to give the reader/listener a clearer picture. In Activity 1, pupils will realise that more than one of the listed words will be suitable adjectives for the nouns. In Activity 2, ask pupils to cover their drawings before sharing them with the class. Discuss the pupils' drawings and decide if all are appropriate. Question 3 may be completed individually or as a class exercise.

Ideas for further practice

- Discuss why some of the adjectives in Question 1 are more suitable than others; for example, 'fresh' or 'stale' would better describe the quality of carrots than 'young' or 'old'.

    These words are more often associated with animals and people.

- Write headings of different kinds of adjectives on the board. Pupils brainstorm to list words that can be used as appropriate adjectives.

    Example:

    Adjectives that describe the **colour** of things (a **white** cat); Adjectives that describe the **size** of things (a **huge** elephant).

Answers

1. The following are suitable answers.
    (a) carrot: crunchy, orange, long
    (b) tiger: fierce, striped, old, young
    (c) hair: shiny, orange, long, curly
    (d) truck: shiny, orange, long, wide, old
    (e) lady: tall, kind, old, young

2. Possible answers: ocean waves during a storm, a shark, a crocodile, a racing car

3. Possible answers:
    (a) winding, dusty, long; old, tumbledown, lonely
    (b) huge, scary, timid; loud, scary, soft
    (c) red, green, juicy, crunchy, ripe, crisp, shiny; juicy, large, seedless, delicious

Adjectives - 2

> An **adjective** is a describing word. It is important to choose the correct words to describe something.

1. Choose the best adjectives from the box to describe the things below. You can choose more than one word.

crunchy	wide	tall	curly
shiny	fierce	orange	striped
long	old	kind	young

(a) carrot _____

(b) tiger _____

(c) hair _____

(d) truck _____

(e) lady _____

2. Draw something that matches these adjectives.

dangerous	quick	greyish

I have drawn _____.

3. Choose adjectives to complete the sentences. Try to make them more interesting.

(a) I walked slowly along the _____ road that led to the

_____ farmhouse.

(b) The _____ giant had a _____ voice.

(c) We bought two _____ apples and a _____ watermelon.

Parts of speech
Adjectives

Focus

Comparative and superlative adjectives

Definitions

- **Comparative adjectives** are used to compare two things, usually using the suffix **er**.

  Example:

  brave, braver

  bad, worse

- **Superlative adjectives** are used to compare more than two things, usually using the suffix **est**.

  Example:

  tall, tallest

  bad, worst

Explanation

- If the adjective has two or more syllables, 'more' or 'most' is usually added before the adjective.

  Example:

  *wonderful, **more** wonderful, **most** wonderful*

- But if adjective of two or more syllables ends in **y**, the **y** turns into **i** and **er** or **est** is usually used.

  Example:

  *nasty, nast**ier**, nast**iest***

Worksheet information

- The words used for comparison in Questions 1 and 2 only include words requiring **er** or **est**. Discuss with the pupils how to add **er** or **est** to adjectives to compare things. Use qualities about pupils or objects in the classroom to teach the concept.

  Example:

  *Identify three pupils—a pupil with **long** hair, a pupil with **longer** hair and a pupil with the **longest** hair.*

- Read and discuss the report about weather in Question 1 with the pupils, identifying how **er** is used at the end of the adjective when two things are compared and **est** is used with three or more things. Note how 'the' is often used before the superlative form (***the wettest day***).

- Pupils answer the questions about weather in Question 2, which provides further practice in using comparatives and superlatives.

- In Question 3, pupils need to add **er** or **est** to a base word. Remind them of the rule that **er** is comparing two things and **est** is used to compare three or more things. They will also need to change the **y** to **i** when adding **er** and **est** to 'shiny' and 'curly'.

Ideas for further practice

- Pupils find pictures in magazines or draw their own to compile a comparison display chart for the class. This activity will probably expose them to the comparative forms (using 'more' and 'most' instead of **er** and **est**).

  Example:

  *They may find a **cheerful** baby, a **more cheerful** baby and the **most cheerful** baby to glue and label on the correct column on the chart.*

- In groups of three, pupils could sort themselves into categories.

  Example:

  *The first making a **soft** sound, the second making a **softer** sound and the third making the **softest** sound.*

  Objects in or outside the classroom could also be used.

Answers

1. wet, deep, dark, cold, wetter, deeper, darker, colder, wettest, deepest, darkest, coldest

2. (a) Monday   (b) Wednesday
   (c) Saturday   (d) Wednesday
   (e) Saturday   (f) Saturday

3. (a) My dad has a ***shiny*** car but Uncle Dan's is ***shinier***.

   (b) Jade has ***curly, brown*** hair. Lisa's hair is ***curlier*** and ***browner***. But Hayley's hair is the ***curliest*** and the ***brownest***.

Comparing things

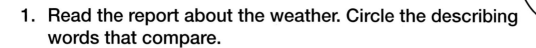

When we compare two or more things we sometimes
add *er* or *est* to a word.

For example:

A kitten is small.

A mouse is small*er*.

An ant is the small*est*.

ADJECTIVES

1. **Read the report about the weather. Circle the describing words that compare.**

Monday was a wet day. There were deep puddles everywhere. The sky was dark and the wind was cold.

Wednesday was a wetter day. The puddles had become deeper. The sky was even darker and the wind was colder.

Saturday was the wettest day. The puddles were the deepest they had been. The sky was the darkest it had been all week and the wind was the coldest.

2. **Answer the questions about the weather.**

   (a)   Which day was wet? _____

   (b)   Which day was wetter? _____

   (c)   Which was the wettest day? _____

   (d)   When had the puddles become deeper? _____

   (e)   When was the sky the darkest? _____

   (f)   When was the wind the coldest? _____

3. **Use the words given to complete the sentences. You will have to add *er* or *est* to some of them.**

   (a)   **shiny**

      My dad has a _____ car but Uncle Dan's is _____.

   (b)   **curly, brown**

      Jade has _____, _____ hair. Lisa's hair is _____

      and _____. But Hayley's hair is the _____ and the

      _____.

Parts of speech

Adverbs

Focus

Common adverbs of manner

Definition

- An **adverb** is a word that adds information, usually to a verb and can tell how (manner), when (time) or where (place) something happens.

  Example:

  *She searched **anxiously** for her car keys. (an adverb of manner)*

  Note: Adverbs can modify (add information to) any words that are not nouns or pronouns.

Explanation

- Adverbs clarify meaning by telling more about the action, allowing for greater precision and adding interest to writing.

- Because of the connection between verbs and adverbs, it is difficult not to discuss or identify adverbs without reference to the verbs they modify. For this reason, the verbs in the text are all bold italic.

- Encourage pupils to use the word 'adverb' and remind them that adding adverbs makes verbs more informative and interesting.

Worksheet information

- Read the text to the pupils, and discuss different things crocodiles do.

- Read the text with the pupils. Point out the words in bold italics and ask them what these words have in common and why they have been highlighted in this way. (They are all verbs or doing words.)

- Revise verbs. (See pages 6–11)

- Explain that the word in the box to the right of each sentence is the answer to a 'How?' question about the verb.

- Model some questions and answers.

  Example:

  *How do you **slip** into the murky water?*

  *I **slip** easily into the murky water.*

- Select pupils to model some questions and answers.

- Explain that words telling how something happens are called adverbs.

- Pupils work with a partner to ask and answer all the questions as modelled.

- Explain to pupils the link between verbs and adverbs in the sentences.

- Before pupils complete Question 1(b), discuss the placement of adverbs and explain that they don't always have to be at the end of a sentence. Encourage them to put the adverbs where they think they sound best.

- Explain that for Question 2 they should look at all the adverbs before selecting the one they think is the best.

- Provide opportunities for pupils, after they have completed Question 3, to share their answers with the class, using complete sentences.

  Example:

  I wish I could dance perfectly.

Ideas for further practice

- Pupils, in groups of 3–5, select a card with an adverb of manner written on it; for example: **politely**, **happily**, **bravely**. They then write the adverb and a list of things they could do in this manner on a large sheet of paper using a felt-tip pen.

  The card and sheet of paper is later passed to another group, so they can add their ideas to the list.

  Provide opportunities for pupils to share their ideas with the class. They should include the adverb each time they read an idea.

  Example:

  'We visit the dentist bravely.' 'We speak politely.'

Answers

Teacher check

Adverbs

1. (a) Read the sentences and the words in the boxes.

I **slip** into murky water. (How?)

I **glide** from place to place. (How?)

I **float** near the top of the water. (How?)

I **pretend** I'm a log. (How?)

I **wait** for my dinner. (How?)

I **leap** out of the water. (How?)

I **snap** my jaws. (How?)

I **grab** my dinner. (How?)

I **eat** it. (How?)

easily
silently
dangerously
cleverly
patiently
suddenly
powerfully
hungrily
greedily

ADVERBS

Words that tell us how things happen are called *adverbs*.

(b) Choose three of the shorter sentences to write. Use the adverbs in your sentences.

_____

_____

_____

2. Choose an adverb from the box to tell how you do these things.

sadly	poorly	politely	loudly	happily	softly
badly	strongly	regularly	beautifully	neatly	well

(a) I swim _____. (b) I smile _____.

(c) I speak _____. (d) I play ball games _____.

(e) I yell _____. (f) I draw _____.

3. Write some things you wish you could do *perfectly*.

Parts of speech

Adverbs

Focus

Common adverbs of manner, time and place

Definition

- An **adverb** is a word that adds information, usually to a verb and can tell about how (manner), when (time) or where (place) something happens.

  Example:

  > **Tomorrow (time)** *we'll* **hopefully (manner)** *find* **somewhere (place)** *to live.*

  Note: Adverbs can modify any words that are not nouns or pronouns.

Explanation

- Adverbs of manner, time and place clarify meaning by telling more about the action, allowing for greater precision and adding interest to writing.

- Because of the connection between verbs and adverbs, it is difficult not to discuss or identify adverbs without reference to the verbs they modify. For this reason, pupils are required to underline the verbs in Question 1 before identifying the adverbs.

- Encourage pupils to use the word 'adverb' and remind them that adding adverbs makes verbs more informative and interesting.

Worksheet information

- Discuss what happens during a storm and encourage pupils to tell their experiences. Revise verbs and make a list of those used by pupils during their recounts.

- Read the sentences in Question 1 with the pupils. Identify and underline the verbs. Explain that sometimes a verb has two words, such as in 'is raining' and 'am snuggled'. (See verbs—pages 6–11.)

- Using 'how', 'when' and 'where' to ask a question will be challenging for many pupils as some of these words will need auxiliary words (such as 'does' and 'do') to be added. Repeated modelling and practice in asking these questions may be required.

  Example:

> *How does the sky change?*
> *When do I see lightning?*
> *Where am I?*

  Note: The verb and/or the word order may also need changing.

- The adverbs in Question 2 are identified in bold to assist pupils to concentrate on classifying them. They should be encouraged to first question whether each adverb tells **how** something happened, and if it doesn't, to then try **when** and, finally, **where**.

- Provide opportunities for pupils to share their answers for Question 3, particularly those not listed on the worksheet.

Ideas for further practice

- Small groups of pupils select a card with a word that can be used as an adverb written on it and have to compile a list of 'What could happen like this?'.

  Example:

  > *'dangerously' – drive, ride, cross the road, dive,*

Answers

1. (a) changes (verb) rapidly (adverb)
   (b) blows (verb) furiously (adverb)
   (c) is raining (verb) already (adverb)
   (d) is (verb) everywhere (adverb)
   (e) see (verb) Now (adverb)
   (f) flashes (verb) dangerously (adverb)
   (g) am (verb) here (adverb)
   (h) am snuggled (verb) safely (adverb)

2. (a) where   (b) when
   (c) when   (d) how

3. Teacher check

How, when and where things happen

ADVERBS

1. Underline the verbs in each line. Ask yourself the questions about the verbs, then write the adverb answers in the boxes.

   The storm

   (a) The sky rapidly changes to black.   How?

   (b) The wind blows furiously.   How?

   (c) It is already raining.   When?

   (d) Water is everywhere.   Where?

   (e) Now I see lightning.   When?

   (f) It flashes dangerously.   How?

   (g) But I am here.   Where?

   (h) I am snuggled safely in my cosy bed.   How?

   > **Words that tell how, when and where things happen are called *adverbs*.**

2. Are these adverbs telling us how, where or when?

   (a) We get violent winter storms **here**.   _____

   (b) There is **often** snow and ice.   _____

   (c) The wind **usually** blows for days.   _____

   (d) Our windows rattle **loudly**.   _____

3. Write an adverb to tell more about the verb in each sentence. You can choose one from the box or think of one yourself.

   (a) The wind is whistling _____ around the house.

   (b) The snow has been falling _____ all night.

   (c) I _____ enjoy walking in the rain.

   (d) Lightning flashed _____.

everywhere	outside	steadily	dangerously	often
softly	noisily	loudly	above	never	sometimes

Parts of speech
Pronouns

Focus

Personal pronouns: emphatic, reflexive

Definitions

- A **pronoun** is a word substituted for a noun.
- A **personal pronoun** is used in place of a person or thing.
- An **emphatic-personal pronoun** emphasises the subject of a verb.

  Example:

  *I will do the work **myself**.*

- A **reflexive-personal pronoun** is the object of the verb.

  Example:

  *They congratulated **themselves**.*

Explanation

- It is important for pupils to know the correct pronouns to use in the context of any sentence so that their grammar, in speech and in writing, is accurate.
- The use of pronouns prevents constant repetition of a noun, making the text more manageable and fluid. As pupils learn the correct pronouns to use, they must also understand which noun a pronoun is replacing.
- Within a sentence, a pronoun performs the same role as a noun, indicating the subject and the object of a verb.

  Example:

  ***I** (subject) hope **you** (object) are happy.*

- There are four types of personal pronoun: subjective and objective (**I** like **you**), possessive (It is **mine**), emphatic (You can do it **yourself**) and reflexive (They saw **themselves**).

- A **possessive personal pronoun** is used to indicate possession of the noun.

  Example:

  *This book is **yours**.*

- An **emphatic-personal pronoun** emphasises the **subject** of a verb and has a different form for each person of the verb.

  Example:

  ***He** (subject) performed the task **himself**.*

  A reflexive personal pronoun is the **object** of the verb and is the same person as the subject. There is a different form of reflexive personal pronoun for each person of the verb.

- The emphatic-reflexive pronouns in the first person are: **myself**, **ourselves**; second person: **yourself**, **yourselves**; and third person: **himself**, **herself**, **itself**, **themselves**.

Note: **Possessive determiners** are not pronouns because they do not replace the noun.

Example:

  *I lost **my** book.*

The possessive determiners in the first person are: **my**, **our**; in the second person: **your**; and in the third person: **his**, **her**, **its**, **their**.

Worksheet information

- Read through the text, identifying and discussing each pronoun. There are examples of subjective personal pronouns (e.g. you, we, it), objective personal pronouns (e.g. me, it, us), possessive personal pronouns (e.g. him, hers) and emphatic-reflexive personal pronouns (herself, myself, ourselves), but pupils do not need to name them at this stage.

Ideas for further practice

- On card, draw a large 4 x 4 chart similar to that in Question 3. On small pieces of card (to fit each cell of the chart), write all the subjective, objective, possessive and emphatic-reflexive pronouns for each category of person (i.e. first, second and third person—singular and plural).

  Pupils work in pairs or small groups to correctly arrange the pronouns for four chosen categories. For each one, they say a sentence which includes that pronoun.

- Write each of the eight emphatic-reflexive pronouns on strips of card. Prepare a series of sentences with one of the pronouns at the end of each sentence. Divide the class into eight groups and distribute the eight cards. Read through each sentence, leaving out the final word. The group holding the card with that pronoun holds up the card and says the word aloud.

- Over the course of one day, pupils note each time they hear an emphatic pronoun (in the classroom). Discuss the context of each example.

Answers

1. (a) you, me   (b) him
   (c) I, it, myself   (d) you, me
   (e) you, it, yourself   (f) you
   (g) hers, she, it, herself   (h) you, us
   (i) it, mine   (j) we, it, ourselves

2. (a) himself   (b) themselves
   (c) ours, yours

3.

I	me	mine	myself
she	her	hers	herself
we	us	ours	ourselves
they	them	theirs	themselves

Myself, yourself

PRONOUNS

Pronouns are words that can be used instead of nouns.

1. Circle the pronouns in the text.

    (a) 'Will you help me bake a cake?'
         asked Dad.

    (b) The rude boy did not even reply
         to him.

    (c) 'Then I shall do it myself', said
         Dad.

    (d) 'Will you help me clear the table?'
         his sister asked.

    (e) 'No! You can do it yourself!' the rude boy replied.

    (f) 'Will you help Mum tidy the garden?' asked Dad.

    (g) 'No! It is hers, she can do it herself!' the rude boy replied.

    (h) 'Will you help us eat the cake?' asked Dad.

    (i) 'Oh yes! Some of it is mine', the rude boy replied.

    (j) 'Oh no!' said Dad. 'We will eat it all ourselves!'

2. Choose a pronoun for each sentence.

yours	himself	ours	themselves

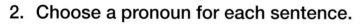

    (a) Dad had to bake the cake _____ .

    (b) The rude boy let his family do all the work _____ .

    (c) 'This cake is _____ , not _____ ',
         said the rude boy's sister.

3. Write the pronouns in the correct place in the table.

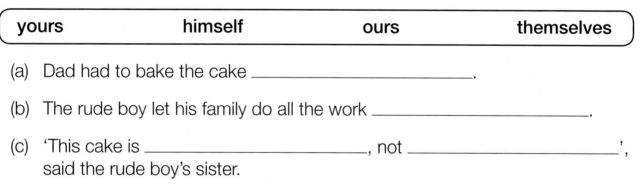

they	us	themselves	she	hers	ours

I		me	mine	myself
		her		herself
	we			ourselves
		them	theirs	

Parts of speech

Pronouns

Focus

Interrogative pronouns

Definition

- **Interrogative pronouns** are those that ask questions and prompt a noun or pronoun reply.

Explanation

- The use of pronouns prevents constant repetition of a noun, making the text more manageable and fluid. As pupils learn the correct pronouns to use, they must also understand which noun a pronoun is replacing.

- There are five interrogative pronouns: **what**, **which**, **who**, **whose** and **whom.**

  Example:

  > **What** *do you want for lunch? A sandwich.*

  > **Which** *filling would you prefer? Salmon and cucumber.*

  Note: **Which** implies a specific choice.

  Who is used when the answer is a subject noun or pronoun.

  > **Who** *wrote this story? James did.*

  Note: **Who** and **whom** refer only to people.

  Whose is used when the answer is a possessive noun or pronoun.

  > **Whose** *is this chair? It's Ben's.*

  Whom is used when the answer is an objective noun or pronoun.

  > **Whom** *did you see at the park? I saw Sally.*

Worksheet information

- Pupils of this age will not appreciate the difference between interrogative pronouns and other words such as 'how', 'when' and 'why', which also ask questions. It is sufficient that they understand that a 'who' question gives a 'person' answer and a 'what' question gives a 'thing' answer.

- The activity is designed for pupils to recognise that the responses to 'who' questions are always people and to 'what' questions are things.

Ideas for further practice

- Play circle games such as 'Who put the cookie in the cookie jar' and an adaptation of 'I went to Paris and I bought … ' where each person is asked one by one by the circle, 'Who are you?' and 'What did you buy?' After each personal response, the pupil is asked about the previous three people: 'Who is he/she?' and 'What did he/she buy?'

- Make fashion booklets using photographs of models in department store advertisements. At the top of each page, pupils write the questions 'Who is this?' and 'What is he/she wearing?' At the foot of the page, pupils make up a name for the model and describe the clothes he/she is wearing.

- Make a selection of cards to use in the game 'Pairs'. On one card is a picture of a person or group of people (use a mixture of famous people and peers, teachers and parents). The second card is an object related to the person or group.

  Example:

  > *Goldilocks – bowl of porridge*

  Each time a card is turned over, ask the questions 'Who is he/she?' or 'Who are they?' for a person/ people card and 'What is this?' or 'What are these?' for an object(s) card. When a matching pair is picked, the pupil collects the cards.

Answers

Teacher check

'Who?' and 'What?'

A *who* question gives a 'person' answer.
A *what* question gives a 'thing' answer.

1. Answer the questions to complete your fact file.

Who are you?	
Who are the people in your family?	
Who are your friends?	
Who sits next to you in class?	
What fruit do you like to eat?	
What sports do you like to play?	
What books do you like to read?	

2. Write some *who* and *what* questions to add to the fact file.

Remember to put a question mark at the end of each question.

Who _____

_____

Who _____

_____

What _____

_____

What _____

_____

Parts of speech

Conjunctions

Focus

Conjunctions

Definition

- **Conjunctions** are joining words which can be used to connect words, phrases or sentences.

  Example:

    salt **and** pepper

    a fast car **but** difficult to control

    finding it difficult **but** continuing to try

    The man carried an umbrella **because** he thought it might rain.

Explanation

- Using conjunctions enables a writer to build and combine ideas and to avoid needless repetition.

  Conjunctions can join:

  - one word with another, such as:
    black **and** white

  - one adjective with another, such as:
    The boat was long **and** sleek.

  - one sentence with another, such as:
    It was my party **so** I cut the cake.

Worksheet information

- Remind pupils to remove the full stops and capital letters when joining sentences in Question 1.

- Most pupils will be familiar with the conjunctions 'and' and 'but'; however, they may need more time and some oral examples to identify 'as', 'when', 'so' and 'or' as conjunctions in the text.

Ideas for further practice

- Pupils create and say a clause which ends in a conjunction (similar to Question 2) and a friend says a suitable ending to complete the sentence.

- View a newspaper or magazine article. Identify and circle the conjunctions.

- Write a sentence which includes a conjunction— because, although, while etc.

Answers

1. (a) The dog looked fierce **but** it was tame.
   (b) Sam grazed his knee **when** he fell off the swing.
   (c) The girl was running **because** she was late.
   (d) I sang **while** I rode my bike.

2. Teacher check: The conjunctions are: because, when and so.

3. 'What was that?' whispered Emma, **as** she pulled the sleeping bag up to her chin **and** shuffled closer to her sister.

   'Well, it could be an owl, **but** we are safe in the back garden, Emma', replied Ava.

   The girls had finally settled down to sleep **when** a scratching noise made them both jump **and** huddle together.

   'It's only me', said Mum, **as** she poked her head through the tent flap. 'I've brought you a torch **so** you won't be scared in the dark.'

Conjunctions

A **conjunction** is a joining word which can be used to join words, groups of words or sentences.

1. Join these sentences by choosing the best conjunction from the words in brackets. Rewrite each sentence.

   For example:

Amy went inside.	It was raining.	(and/because)

   Amy went inside **because** it was raining.

   (a) The dog looked fierce.   It was tame.   (if/but)

   _____

   (b) Sam grazed his knee.   He fell off the swing.   (when/while)

   _____

   (c) The girl was running.   She was late.   (because/but)

   _____

   (d) I sang.   I rode my bike.   (and/while)

   _____

2. Finish each sentence in your own words. Underline the conjunctions.

   (a) I had a bath because _____.

   (b) We left the park when _____.

   (c) My hair was too long so _____.

3. (a) Read the text.

   '*What was that?*' *whispered Emma, as she pulled the sleeping bag up to her chin and shuffled closer to her sister.*

   '*Well, it could be an owl, but we are safe in the back garden, Emma*', *replied Ava.*

   The girls had finally settled down to sleep when a scratching noise made them both jump and huddle together.

   '*It's only me*', *said Mum, as she poked her head through the tent flap.* '*I have brought you a torch so you won't be scared in the dark.*'

   (b) Find the seven conjunctions in the text and circle them.

Parts of speech
Determiners

Focus

Articles: **the** (definite) and **a/an** (indefinite)

Demonstratives: **this, that** (singular) and **these, those** (plural)

Definitions

- A **determiner** is a word usually used before a noun that determines how definite it is.

  Example:

  > **That** train with **some** empty carriages is travelling along **the** tracks and stopping at **each** station.

- An **article** is a type of **determiner** that precedes a noun and identifies how definite (specific) or indefinite (non-specific) that noun is.

  Example:

  > *a* book (meaning any book), **the** book (meaning a particular book)

- A **demonstrative** is a type of determiner that signals whether the associated noun is **near** (this, these) the writer or speaker, or **far away** (that, those) from the writer or speaker.

  Note: In traditional grammar, some words used as what are now called **determiners** in functional grammar are referred to as **adjectives**; e.g. *first, seven,* or as **possessive pronouns**; e.g. *my, your*.

Explanation

- Determiners are useful for making information more precise for the reader or listener.

- The definite article **the** is used to refer to a particular thing or things. **The** is used when referring to specific, one-of-a-kind things.

  Example:

  > **the** *Nile River,* **the** *book* (meaning a particular book)

- Indefinite articles such as **a** and **an** are used to refer to any thing. The noun following an indefinite article is non-specific.

  Example:

  > *an* umbrella (meaning any umbrella), or *a* boat (meaning any boat)

- Articles can indicate a significant difference in meaning.

Example:

> *a* house (any house), **the** house (a particular house)

- The indefinite article **a** precedes a noun that begins with a consonant sound.

  Example:

  > *a* yacht, *a* boat, *a* dog, *a* unicycle

- The indefinite article **an** precedes a noun that begins with a vowel sound.

  Example:

  > *an* apple, *an* ice-cream, *an* umbrella, *an* hour

- Demonstratives generally indicate the proximity of the noun to the writer or speaker. **This** (singular) and **these** (plural) suggest the noun/nouns are close by, while **that** (singular) and **those** (plural) suggest the noun/nouns is/are far away or out of reach.

Worksheet information

- Question 1 provides a simple text for discussion about the use of **a**, **an** and **the**. Direct pupils to observe the instances in which **a** or **an** are used (with consonant sounds or vowel sounds). Discuss and establish a class list of words which use the determiner **a** and words which use *an*. **The** can be used with any word as it identifies the specific nature of the noun.

- Pupils then complete Question 2 independently.

- Read the sentences in Question 3 and discuss the words in bold print. Identify that the pupils understand that these words tell about proximity. If not, point this feature out explicitly. Pupils then match the sentences to the pictures independently.

Ideas for further practice

- Pupils write a limerick incorporating 'a', 'an' and 'the'.

- Pupils create his/her own sentences which demonstrate the correct use of 'this', 'that', 'these' and 'those'.

Answers

2. a: cat, mouse; an: apple, owl; the: sky, water

3. (a) 2   (b) 3   (c) 4   (d) 1

What do the words tell us?

1. Read this limerick.

*There was **an old man** on the moon*
*who liked to sing **a tune**.*
It made him quite sad
*to find **the atmosphere** was bad*
and no-one could hear him croon!

The words in ***bold print*** tell us more about the noun. The words 'an' and 'a' tell us that it could be any ***old*** man singing any ***tune***! 'The' tells us that it is a particular ***moon*** with a particular ***atmosphere***.

2. Sort the nouns below into groups.

sky	cat	apple	water	owl	mouse

a	an	the

3. Match the sentences to the correct picture. The words in bold print will help you.

(a) **Those** cats are very playful.　　**1**

(b) **These** cats are very sleepy.　　**2**

(c) **This** ball is very bouncy.　　**3**

(d) **That** ball is very flat.　　**4**

Parts of speech
Determiners

Focus

Possessive determiners: **my, your, his, her, its, our, their**

Definitions

- A **determiner** is a word usually used before a noun that determines how definite it is.

  Example:

  *Your family lived in **that** house with **some** tall trees which dropped lots of leaves in **the** garden **each** year.*

- A **possessive determiner** is a word which identifies who something belongs to.

  Example:

  *Mary sold **her** book at the fete.*

  Note: In traditional grammar, some words used as what are now called **determiners** in functional grammar are referred to as **adjectives**; e.g. *first, seven*, or as **possessive pronouns**; e.g. *my, your*.

Explanation

- Determiners are useful for making information more precise for the reader or listener.

- Possessive determiners are always used before the noun to say who the noun belongs to. They can be used in first, second or third person as well as singular or plural. Refer to the table below to see which possessive determiners are used in each situation.

	Person	Determiner	Pronoun
Singular	1st	my	I, me, mine
	2nd	your	you, yours
	3rd	his	he, him, his
		her	she, her, hers
		its	it, its
Plural	1st	our	we, us, ours
	2nd	your	you, yours
	3rd	their	they, them, theirs

Note: **Possessive proper nouns** are determiners.

Example:

Deb's work

Worksheet information

- Introduce several examples of possessive determiners from the table. Have each word on a flash card, display the word and ask a pupil to give an oral sentence which uses the word. Listen carefully to the sentence, then provide feedback as to the correct or incorrect use of the word. If incorrect, provide a correct version of the sentence. Questions 1 and 2 provide opportunities to discuss that some possessives are suitable for plural or singular and some for masculine and feminine.

- Read the sentences in Question 3. Identify the relationship between the missing word and the underlined word (plural–plural, singular–singular).

  Example:

  'Molly lost their kitten on the weekend' would not work because *'Molly'* is singular feminine and *'their'* is plural generic. The correct missing word to use in this instance is *'her'*, it being singular and feminine.

Ideas for further practice

- Create a class book with chapters. Each chapter is dedicated to a particular possessive determiner. Divide the class into seven groups (one for each determiner) and have each pupil write a sentence which incorporates his/her particular word. Draw a picture to match. Collate the pages into the appropriate chapters, produce a contents page and a cover.

- Have pupils write labels to display around the class; for example, Alisha's chair.

Answers

1. Singular: my, your, his, its, her
   Plural: our, your, their

2. Masculine: his
   Feminine: her
   Both: my, your, its, our, their

3. (a) her   (b) my   (c) our
   (d) his   (e) Your   (f) their
   (g) its

Who does it belong to?

1. **The words in the table tell us who something belongs to.**

   Read each word and decide whether it is used to show 'ownership by one' (singular) or 'ownership by many' (plural).

   Tick the correct box.

word	singular	plural
my		
our		
your		
his		
its		
her		
their		

2. **Now look at the words in the table again.**

   (a) Colour the words which can only be used for boys (masculine) in blue.

   (b) Colour the words which can only be used for girls (feminine) in red.

   (c) Colour the words which can be used for boys or girls in yellow.

3. **Use these words to complete the sentences.**

their	our	my	your	its	her	his

   The <u>underlined</u> words will give you a clue as to which words to use!

   (a) <u>Molly</u> lost _____ kitten on the weekend.

   (b) 'Would you like to come to _____ house to play?' I asked.

   (c) <u>We</u> found a frog in _____ garden.

   (d) <u>Brady</u> read _____ book to the teacher.

   (e) <u>I</u> am very proud of <u>you</u>. _____ homework is very neat.

   (f) It is _____ turn to pack away the paints. <u>They</u> didn't do it last week.

   (g) The <u>cat</u> likes to lick _____ paws after eating.

Parts of speech
Prepositions

Focus

Prepositions

Definition

- **Prepositions** are words used to show the relationship between nouns and/or pronouns in the same sentence.

  Example:

  *The rugby player ran **across** the park **with** the ball tucked tightly **under** his arm.*

Explanation

- The word 'preposition' combines the prefix **pre** (meaning 'before' or 'in front of') and the word **position**. As such, prepositions are words that are **positioned in front** of nouns or other words that functions as nouns (such as pronouns, verbal nouns or noun phrases).

- Prepositions indicate a connection between things mentioned in a sentence, such as between a person and where she/he is going.

  Example:

  *Jill moved **towards** the table.*

  Prepositions can refer to manner *(he came to work **by** bus)*, time *(school starts **at** 9 am)*, place *(he left his shoes **at** the park)*, position *(the cat lay **under** the table)*, and direction *(it ran **between** the buildings)*. Some prepositions are formed by combining words, such as the phrases **in front of**, **on top of** and **prior to**.

- Prepositions are often used to introduce phrases that add more information to the noun or verb. These are called **prepositional phrases**. These phrases start with a preposition and end with a noun or noun equivalent (called the 'object' of the preposition). Words that modify the object are part of the phrase.

  Example:

  *'The **girl** (subject), though tall, was still shorter **than** (preposition) her **younger brother** (object).'*
  (The prepositional phrase is underlined.)

- As a rule, prepositions do not come before verbs. An old rule with prepositions was that they should never end a sentence. This was based on the fact that the traditional rules of English grammar were taken from Latin, and in Latin it is not possible to end a sentence with a preposition. This rule no longer applies. For example, it is commonly accepted as

correct to say *'Have you found the shoes you were looking **for**?'* (Rather than the Old English: *'Have you found the shoes **for** which you were looking?'*)

- Prepositions add meaning and detail. They also help to distinguish between the object and the subject in a sentence. Commonly used prepositions include **about, above, across, after, against, around, at, before, behind, beneath, beside, between, beyond, by, for, from, in, inside, near, off, on, out, over, through, to, toward, under, until, upon** and **with**. Bear in mind that these words are not always prepositions; sometimes they function as conjunctions or adverbs.

  Example:

  *Mia decided to stay **inside**.*

  'Inside' has no object and so is an adverb.

Worksheet information

- Giving directions is good practice for using position prepositions. After each pupil has been given a copy of the worksheet, read the text with them. Discuss prepositions and how they give us information about where things are.

  Ask pupils to give examples, based on the worksheet, of using the prepositions, such as *'The creepy cave is **under** the mountains, **next** to Eel River'*.

- Pupils draw an 'X' on the page where they would like the treasure to be. They then plot a route to the treasure and write down the directions, using as many prepositions as possible. Pupils then draw their own treasure map on the back of the sheet, or on a separate sheet of paper, using prepositions once again to give directions to the treasure.

Ideas for further practice

- Pupils can pretend to be tourists or new pupils at the school and practise giving directions to each other.

- Pupils could draw maps of their neighbourhood and use them to describe how they get to school each day.

- Make treasure hunt clues for small groups of children to find a treasure at school.

  Example:

  Give one group a piece of paper that says *'Look **in** the bookshelf'*, and in the bookshelf put another clue that says *'Look **inside** the dictionary'* etc.

Where is the treasure?

Words that tell us about where people, places and things are, or are going, are called **prepositions**.

Words like *above, along, around, at, behind, below, beside, between, down, into, in front of, from, near, on, out, over, past, through, towards* and *under* are prepositions.

1. Draw an 'X' on the map where you think the treasure is hidden.

2. Write at least five instructions to get to the treasure from 'Start'. Use as many prepositions as you can.

_____

_____

_____

_____

_____

_____

3. On the back of this sheet, draw your own treasure map. The map can be of a park, zoo, shopping centre or school. Use prepositions to write instructions for how to find the treasure.

Understanding and choosing words

Homographs

Focus

Homographs

Definition

- **Homographs** are words that are spelt the same but have different meanings.

  Example:

    tap – *a device used to control the flow of water*

    tap – *to touch lightly, as on the shoulder*

  Sometimes homographs are pronounced differently.

  Example:

    bow *(rhymes with* **cow***) – to bend or stoop down to an audience*

    bow *(rhymes with* **toe***) – a knot with two hoops and two ends/the playing stick used with a violin*

Explanation

- Recognising and using different homographs develops and enriches pupils' vocabulary. They learn to understand the meaning of words and the way they work in print.

Worksheet information

- As an introduction, give two 'What am I?' clues to the pupils to demonstrate two different meanings for the same word.

  Example:

    Clue 1: *I am long and grey. I am found on an elephant. I am a type of nose.*

    Clue 2: *I am made of wood. I am the main part of a tree.*

  Ask them to guess the word and discuss the different meanings. Pupils may suggest other meanings for 'trunk', such as a chest for storing possessions or the main part of the human body.

- Complete Question 1 on the worksheet and discuss the pupils' answers as a class.

- In the crossword in Question 2, pairs of clues have the same word (homograph) as the answer. The different meanings for each word pair could be made more obvious to the pupils if they colour-code the two clues and the words in the crossword the same colour. Discuss any other meanings pupils suggest for any of the words.

- The word 'tear' is an example of a homograph that has different pronunciations. Discuss this with the pupils before they complete Question 3.

Ideas for further practice

- Pupils compile a class homograph chart for reference. A word can be written with two or more sentences underneath giving different meanings. The word can be written in a different colour to stand out. It may be useful to illustrate the meaning of some words as well.

- Hold a competition to see which group can come up with the most meanings for a homograph.

Answers

1. (a) a deep circular dish used to put food or liquid in
   (b) to throw a ball, as in the game of cricket

2. Teacher check highlighted words.

3. (a) to rip
   (b) a drop of water that falls from your eyes

Homographs

Some words are spelt the same but have more than one meaning. They are called **homographs**.

1. The pictures below show two different meanings for the homograph 'bowl'. Write a sentence to explain each meaning.

(a)  _____

_____

(b) _____

_____

2. (a) Complete the crossword.

   (b) Use different coloured highlight pens or pencils to colour the pairs of clues that give the same answer.

Across

1. A long, thin piece of wood.
4. Turn off the _____ and go to sleep.
6. Turn off the water _____.
7. A place where you can keep money.
8. Used to light a fire.
10. A drop of water that falls from your eye.
11. Our dog likes to _____ her head out the car window.

Down

1. There is a dirty _____ on my shirt.
2. The duck waddled up the river _____.
3. I looked but I couldn't _____ him in the crowd.
4. The opposite of heavy.
5. _____ a sheet of paper from your pad.
9. Our football team won the _____.
12. When I'm ready, I'll _____ you on the shoulder.

3. **Did you notice that 'tear' can be pronounced in two ways? Write the different meanings.**

   (a) *tear* (rhymes with *pair*) _____

   (b) *tear* (rhymes with *deer*) _____

Understanding and choosing words

Homophones

Focus

Homophones

Definition

- **Homophones** are words that sound the same but are spelt differently and have different meanings.

  Example:

  threw – *hurled through the air (past tense of the verb 'to throw')*

  through – *to go in at one side and come out the other*

Explanation

- Identifying different homophones and recognising how to spell them helps pupils to communicate more clearly in written form. Investigating homophones also helps to develop and enrich pupils' vocabulary. They learn to understand the meaning of words and the way they work in print.

Worksheet information

- Explain how a word can sound the same as another but be spelt differently and have a different meaning.

  Example:

  Draw a pear on the board and ask pupils what it is. Write the word 'pear' on the board and ask if they can think of another meaning for this word. Give them a hint by pointing to a pair of shoes. Write 'pair' on the board and discuss the different spellings and meanings. Pupils could give other examples of homophones.

- Discuss what the pupils are expected to do on the worksheet. Some pupils will be able to work independently, using a dictionary to help them identify the correct spellings. Discuss the different drawings and sentences for Questions 1 and 3.

Ideas for further practice

- Write words that are homophones on the back of blank playing cards, one word per card. Pupils can play games such as 'Snap' and 'Concentration' where they identify homophone pairs. Alternatively, while playing 'Concentration', pupils have to put each homophone pair in a sentence and have it endorsed by other members in the group or by a teacher/adult helper.

- Make a wordsearch that includes the homophones for a list of given words. Pupils look at a homophone in the list and must locate, highlight and write the homophone next to its pair.

Answers

1. Teacher check

2. Last (**week**/weak), my sister and (eye/**I**) went (**to**/too/two) the (fare/**fair**) on the other side of town. As it was (to/**too**/two) hot to walk, we decided to go (**by**/bye) bus. We made sure we had enough money (**for**/four) (**our**/hour) return (fair/**fare**).

   At the (fare/**fair**), we went on lots of rides. (Eye/**I**) thought Elise (**would**/wood) feel ill if she went on the Rockin Rollercoaster, but she said she (wood/**would**) (**be**/bee) okay. After a few (ours/**hours**), we (**knew**/new) it was time to make (**our**/hour) way home and left the (fare/**fair**) (**to**/too/two) catch the bus.

3. Teacher check

Homophones

Some words sound the same but are spelt differently and have different meanings. They are called *homophones*.

1. Choose one word of each homophone pair and draw a picture to show the meaning of the word. Highlight the word you chose.

(a) saw/sore	(b) red/read

2. Circle or highlight the correct homophone to complete the story.

Last *(week/weak)*, my sister and *(eye/I)* went *(to/too/two)* the *(fare/fair)* on the other side of town. As it was *(to/too/two)* hot to walk, we decided to go *(by/bye/buy)* bus. We made sure we had enough money *(for/four)* *(our/hour)* return *(fair/fare)*.

At the *(fare/fair),* we went on lots of rides. *(Eye/I)* thought Elise *(would/wood)* feel ill if she went on the Rockin' Rollercoaster, but she said she *(wood/would)* *(be/bee)* okay. After a few *(ours/hours)*, we *(knew/new)* it was time to make *(our/hour)* way home and left the *(fare/fair)* *(to/too/two)* catch the bus.

3. Use each word in a sentence to show its meaning.

threw _____

_____

through _____

_____

wear _____

_____

where _____

_____

Understanding and choosing words

Word groups

Focus

Compound words

Definition

- A **compound word** is formed when two words are joined together to make a new word with a different meaning.

Explanation

- In many cases, the meaning of the compound word is related to that of its constituent words.

    Example:

    daytrip – *a trip taken during the day*
- Pupils will have fun identifying and making new words while developing their vocabulary.

Worksheet information

- Prior to completing the sheet, look around the classroom and identify the names of any objects which are compound words.

    Example:

    classroom, whiteboard

    Encourage pupils to suggest any other compound words and discuss the words they are made from.

    Example:

    bumblebee, firefly, butterfly

    Discuss the meanings of all the words, explaining that the compound word has a different meaning from its constituent words although they are usually related.
- With Question 1, read through the text and identify the compound words. Compare the meaning of the compound words and their constituent words. Note that all but 'forward' are related in meaning. For this reason, pupils may find 'forward' less easy to identify.
- With Question 2, pupils read the clues to find the compound words to place in the puzzle.

Ideas for further practice

- Make laminated cards on which a single constituent word of a compound word is written. Use the cards to play games such as 'Snap' and 'Pairs', where each pair must join together to make the compound word.
- Read familiar stories and highlight compound words. On A3 paper, write the title of each story and the compound words found. Compare the meanings of the words to their constituent words. Ask: Which are general high-frequency words? Which are specific to the subject of the story? Hang the words around the classroom on mobiles made from wire coathangers.
- Type 'compound words' into a search engine. Use the variety of activities on offer for pupils to consolidate their knowledge and understanding of compound words and to develop their vocabulary.

Answers

1. (a) Teacher check
   (b) for + ward, week + end, birth + day, camp + site, light + house, bed + time, pan + cakes, camp + fire

2. *Across:* 4. waterfall, 6. teatime, 7. matchbox, 8. dishcloth

   Down: 1. peanut, 2. scarecrow, 3. tablecloth, 5. newspaper

Compound words

1. (a) Underline the compound words in the text.

Tom was looking forward to the weekend. His dad had promised him a special treat for his birthday. They were going to a quiet campsite on the coast, not far from the lighthouse. At bedtime, Tom dreamt of sitting under the stars while his Dad made pancakes on the campfire.

(b) With the words you found, write the two words which make each compound word.

_____ + _____   _____ + _____

_____ + _____   _____ + _____

_____ + _____   _____ + _____

_____ + _____   _____ + _____

2. Answer the clues with a compound word to solve the puzzle.

Across

4. Water falling downwards.
6. Time for tea.
7. Small box to keep matches.
8. Cloth to wash dishes.

Down

1. A small, pea-like nut.
2. To scare away crows.
3. Cloth to put on a table.
5. Paper full of news.

Understanding and choosing words

Word groups

Definition

Alphabetical order is a system used to arrange items so they can be easily found. Alphabetical order is used in many areas with which pupils are familiar.

Example:

the class register, in dictionaries, at the library, the index at the back of a reference book, telephone directories, map books

Explanation

- Initially, words are ordered by the first letter, then the second, third and so on until all words are in correct alphabetical order.

Worksheet information

- Prior to completing the sheet, show pupils examples of how alphabetical order is used in daily life.

Example:

street names in road books, names in telephone directories, indexes at the back of books

- Ask the pupils to line up (girls and boys separately) in alphabetical order. If there are two or more pupils whose name begins with the same letter, explain the second, third etc. letter convention.

- In Question 1, pupils arrange the savoury and sweet food in alphabetical order by first letter.

- In Question 2, pupils arrange the girl and boy names in alphabetical order by first letter.

- In Question 3, pupils arrange the animals on each line in alphabetical order by the second letter.

Ideas for further practice

- Make several lists of words for pupils to place in alphabetical order by first, second or third letter or a mixture of all three. Choose subjects that are of some interest to the pupils.

Example:

sports, TV programmes, popular authors, local place names

- Select words beginning with the same letter from the pupils' dictionaries. Pupils arrange these words in order, then check their list by finding the words in the dictionary.

- Pupils plan quiz questions about different continents, listing some countries, cities and physical features for the rest of the class to arrange in alphabetical order.

Answers

1. (a) Teacher check
   (b) savoury shish kebab: cheese, ham, onion, prawn, tomato
       sweet shish kebab: apple, cherry, grape, melon, orange

2. (a) girls: Bethany, Elise, Melanie, Rita, Tessa
   (b) boys: Andrew, Jack, Robert, Sam, Thomas

3. (a) scorpion, seal, shark
   (b) baboon, beaver, bison
   (c) tiger, toad, turkey
   (d) octopus, otter, owl
   (e) lion, lobster, lynx
   (f) manatee, meerkat, mole

Alphabetical order

a b c d e f g h i j k l m n o p q r s t u v w x y z

1. (a) Draw the food in alphabetical order to make each shish kebab.

   (b) Write the food's name under each picture.

Savoury shish kebab

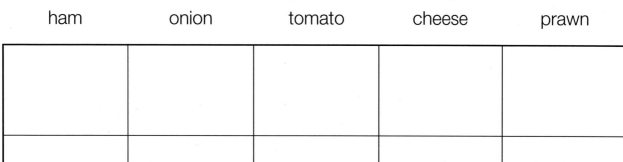

ham	onion	tomato	cheese	prawn

Sweet shish kebab

melon	cherry	apple	orange	grape

2. Arrange the children in alphabetical order.

   (a) **girls:** Rita, Bethany, Tessa, Melanie, Elise

   _____

   (b) **boys:** Jack, Thomas, Andrew, Sam, Robert

   _____

3. Underline the second letter in each word. Use this letter to place the words in alphabetical order.

   (a) shark   scorpion   seal   _____

   (b) beaver   bison   baboon   _____

   (c) turkey   tiger   toad   _____

   (d) otter   owl   octopus   _____

   (e) lynx   lobster   lion   _____

   (f) mole   meerkat   manatee   _____

Understanding and choosing words

Word groups

Focus

The names of different sports

Explanation

- By learning new words, pupils are developing and enriching their vocabulary, and in doing so, they will also be learning how to read and spell the words.

Worksheet information

- For Question 1, pupils read the letter and underline the sports mentioned.

- With Question 2, pupils read the clues and solve them to discover the sports. Remind pupils the answers can be found in the text above.

- Explain to the class that the names of sports are special words called **nouns**.

  Noun: A word used to name things, people, places, feelings or ideas.

  A capital letter is not used to name sports unless it is the name of a sports team. The only time any noun is capitalised is when it is a proper noun. A proper noun refers to a particular person, place or thing.

  Example:

  – *Jason went to a football match.*

  – *Jason went to see Manchester United play football.*

  Refer to pages 2–5 for more information and activities about nouns.

- Ask the pupils to think of other types of sports.

  Example:

  squash, badminton, gymnastics, fencing

Ideas for further practice

- Play the game 'Charades', where the class has to guess the sport a pupil is miming.

- Choose five sports and list and draw the equipment required to play each one.

- In small groups, pupils work together to list sports played at the Olympic Games and Commonwealth Games. Pupils use them to create a wordsearch for a friend to solve.

Answers

1. golf, swimming, bowls, hockey, netball, volleyball, cricket, football, basketball, tennis.

2.

Sports

1. Read the letter and underline the sports mentioned.

Dear Lola

We are here! Dad is very excited as our new house is next door to a golf course. Mum goes swimming every morning in our pool and Nanna has already found a friend to play bowls with.

I can't decide if I will play hockey or netball. My new friend, Stella, has also asked me to join her volleyball team!

As the cricket season is over, Josh has joined the local football team. He is also playing basketball.

The sun is out so we are all off for a hit of tennis this afternoon.

Write soon, love

Madison x

2. Complete the crossword about sports. The answers are in the text above.

Across

4. Players score runs and hit 'fours' and 'sixes'.
5. A small white ball is hit towards a hole, then tapped in.
7. Players try to roll their balls next to the jack.
9. A ball is bounced down a wooden court and thrown into a hoop.
10. Teams hit a ball over a high net using their hands.

Down

1. Breaststroke and butterfly are strokes in this sport.
2. A ball is pushed or hit down a field towards the goal using a hooked stick.
3. Two or four players hit a ball over a net.
6. A ball is kicked and dribbled down a large grass pitch towards the goal.
8. Goal attack, goal keeper and wing attack are positions in this sport.

Understanding and choosing words

Word groups

Focus

The names of the main food groups and some international foods

Explanation

• By learning new words, pupils are developing and enriching their vocabulary, and in doing so, they will also be learning how to read and spell the words.

Worksheet information

• Read the text and discuss the *Healthy eating guide* with the class.

• Pupils complete the sentences in Question 2 by filling in the food groups.

• Pupils need access to a dictionary and the Internet to learn about the foods in the list from Question 3. Pupils can work together to determine which food groups the foods belong to and to sort them accordingly.

• Explain to the class that the names of food are special words called **nouns**.

Noun: A word used to name things, people, places, feelings or ideas.

Refer to pages 2–5 for more information and activities about nouns.

• Ask the pupils to think of other types of international foods not included on the worksheet, such as fruits and vegetables.

Ideas for further practice

• Pupil write a poem which promotes the benefits of eating using the *Healthy eating guide*.

• As a class, create a dinner meal which includes a selection of foods from all of the food groups.

• Pupils list what they have eaten for one whole day and sort the foods into the different food groups. Does their list resemble the *Healthy eating guide*? How can they improve their diet?

• Bring to class breads from different cultures, such as: naan, pitta, ciabatta, Turkish bread, cornbread, baguette etc. Pupils taste and rate the breads.

Answers

2. (a) carbohydrates
   (b) protein
   (c) dairy
   (d) fruit, vegetables
   (e) fats, oils

3.

Carbohydrates	Vegetables/ Fruits	Dairy	Protein
rice	bok choy	ricotta	chicken curry
naan	lychee	gelato	biltong
ciabatta	ackee	soy milk	salmon

Food groups

1. **Read about the *Healthy eating guide*.**

Vegetables and fruit

Eating vegetables and fruit gives you healthy bones, teeth, eyes and skin. It also helps fight obesity.

Carbohydrates

Eating breads, cereals, rice and pasta gives you energy and helps you to grow.

Fats and oils

Only eat oil and fats in small amounts.

Dairy

Eating milk, yoghurt and cheese gives you energy, strong teeth and bones.

Protein

Eating meat, fish, chicken, eggs and nuts helps you to grow and repair your body.

2. **Complete the sentences by adding the correct food group.**

   (a) Bread and pasta are _____ which give you energy.

   (b) Nuts, meat and eggs are all types of _____.

   (c) Have strong bones by eating _____ products such as cheese and milk.

   (d) To stay at a healthy weight, eat lots of _____

   and _____.

   (e) Only eat small amounts of _____ and

   _____.

3. **Sort these international foods into the food groups. Use the *Healthy eating guide*, a dictionary and the Internet to help you complete the table.**

   ricotta   bok choy   rice   naan   ackee   chicken curry

   gelato   salmon   soy milk   ciabatta   biltong   lychee

Carbohydrates	Vegetables/Fruits	Dairy	Protein

Understanding and choosing words

Plurals

Focus

Plurals: adding **s** or **es**

Irregular plurals: words that change

words that stay the same

Definition

- A **plural** is a word used to indicate more than one.
  Example:

  *three **apples**, three **brushes***

Explanation

- 'Singular' means 'one'. 'Plural' means 'more than one'.
- There are many ways to form the plural of a word.
- To form the plural of most nouns, we just add an **s**.
- To form the plural of words ending with **sh**, **ch**, **s** and **x**, we add **es** to make the word easier to pronounce.
- To form the plural of some words, the word changes.
  Example:

  *one **louse** – many **lice***

- Some words have the same form whether the word is singular or plural.
  Example:

  *one **sheep** – many **sheep***

- It is important that pupils realise that there are many exceptions to most spelling rules. They should be encouraged to identify these exceptions and to share them with the class.

Worksheet information

- Once pupils locate the plural form of each word, ask them to underline the **ch**, **s** and **x** at the end of the words to highlight the rule of adding **es**. Ask pupils to think of more animal names which are made plural by adding **es**.
  Example:

  finches, fishes

  You may like to point out to pupils that the plural of 'octopus' is 'octopuses' but may also be 'octopi'. 'Fish' Is another interesting one. The plural is generally 'fish'; however, when referring to many different types of species, the term 'fishes' is used.

- Some plural words change their vowels or use a different suffix to become plural. By using a matching activity, pupils can visually compare the words to see how they change. Ask pupils to circle any changes made from the singular form to the plural form. Discuss these observations.

- Before completing Question 4, discuss how some animal names do not change at all, whether they are singular or plural. Ask pupils to think of more animal names which remain the same.
  Example:

  fish, cattle, salmon, cod, bison, tuna, deer

Ideas for further practice

- Make animal word mobiles. Each mobile contains only animal names which are made plural by each method used on the worksheet.
  Example:

  *One mobile would have only animal names which add **s**, another would have only animals names which add **es**.*

Answers

2. birds, cows, ants, dogs, cats, foxes, octopuses, albatrosses, rhinoceroses, cockroaches

c	a	d	d	e	b	s	s
o	s	t	n	a	i	a	e
c	t	o	w	o	r	l	s
k	r	d	s	c	d	b	o
r	d	s	e	a	s	a	r
o	o	e	s	t	n	t	e
a	g	d	u	s	c	r	c
c	s	i	p	n	o	o	o
h	g	i	o	n	w	s	n
e	s	h	t	c	s	s	i
s	h	s	c	a	n	e	h
d	x	f	o	x	e	s	r

3. Add **es** to words ending in **sh, ch, s** and **x**.

4. mouse – mice   ox – oxen
   goose – geese   louse – lice

5. sheep, tuna, moose, reindeer

Animal, animals and more animals

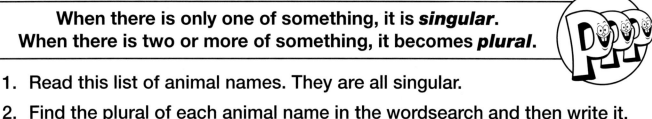

PLURALS

> When there is only one of something, it is *singular*.
> When there is two or more of something, it becomes *plural*.

1. Read this list of animal names. They are all singular.

2. Find the plural of each animal name in the wordsearch and then write it.

bird　＿＿＿＿＿＿＿＿＿＿＿

cow　＿＿＿＿＿＿＿＿＿＿＿

ant　＿＿＿＿＿＿＿＿＿＿＿

dog　＿＿＿＿＿＿＿＿＿＿＿

cat　＿＿＿＿＿＿＿＿＿＿＿

fox　＿＿＿＿＿＿＿＿＿＿＿

octopus　＿＿＿＿＿＿＿＿＿＿＿

albatross　＿＿＿＿＿＿＿＿＿＿＿

rhinoceros　＿＿＿＿＿＿＿＿＿＿＿

cockroach　＿＿＿＿＿＿＿＿＿＿＿

c	a	d	d	e	b	s	s
o	s	t	n	a	i	a	e
c	t	o	w	o	r	l	s
k	r	d	s	c	d	b	o
r	d	s	e	a	s	a	r
o	o	e	s	t	n	t	e
a	g	d	u	s	c	r	c
c	s	i	p	n	o	o	o
h	g	i	o	n	w	s	n
e	s	h	t	c	s	s	i
s	h	s	c	a	n	e	h
d	x	f	o	x	e	s	r

3. Write the leftover letters from top to bottom and left to right to complete this rule to make plural words easier to say.

☐☐☐ '☐☐' ☐☐ ☐☐☐☐☐☐

☐☐☐☐☐☐ ☐☐ '☐☐', '☐☐',

'☐' ☐☐☐ '☐'.

4. Match these words to their plural.

mouse　•　•　oxen
ox　•　•　geese
goose　•　•　lice
louse　•　•　mice

5. Write the missing vowels.

sh ＿＿ ＿＿ p　t ＿＿ na　m ＿＿ os ＿＿　r ＿＿ ＿＿ nd　r

These animal names stay the same whether there is one or many.

Understanding and choosing words

Plurals

PLURALS

Focus

Plurals: words ending with a consonant followed by the letter **y**

words ending with **f**

Definition

- A **plural** is a word used to indicate more than one.
  Example:
  *three **apples**, three **brushes**.*

Explanation

- 'Singular' means 'one'. 'Plural' means 'more than one'.
- There are many ways to form the plural of a word.
- To form the plural of words ending with a consonant and **y**, change the **y** to **i** and add **es**.
  Example:
  *fair**y** – fair**ies***
- To form the plural of words ending in **f**, change the **f** to **v** and add **es**.
  Example:
  *shel**f** – shel**ves***
- It is important that pupils realise that there are many exceptions to most spelling rules. They should be encouraged to identify these exceptions and to share them with the class.

Worksheet information

- After reading the first rule with the pupils, list words to practise the rule. Pupils then complete the activity. Once completed, pupils can write the plural words from the crossword puzzle in sentences on the back of the worksheet or a separate sheet of paper.
- Read the second rule with the pupils and read each word in the box. Read each sentence and ask pupils which word belongs. Read each sentence with the word in its singular form and ask the pupils to listen carefully. The words must be plural in order for the sentences to sound correct. Pupils then complete the sentences.

Note: For some words ending in **f**, we just add **s** to make them plural.
Example:
chiefs, roofs, handkerchiefs, cliffs, puffs

Ideas for further practice

- Pupils create a 'plural dictionary'. Each chapter is devoted to a particular plural rule and lists as many words as they can think of that follow the rule. Encourage pupils to use the dictionary as a reference and to add to it as they discover new rules, exceptions to the rules and new words to fit each rule.

Answers

1.

1.f	a	m	i	l	i	e	2.s
a							t
i				3.p			o
r				u			r
i				p			i
e				p			e
s		4.b	a	b	i	e	s
				e			
5.t	e	d	d	i	e	s	

2. (a) leaves (b) halves (c) shelves
   (d) Thieves (e) wolves

Interesting plurals

Usually when a word ends with a consonant followed by 'y', change the 'y' to 'i' and add 'es' to make it *plural*.

1. Read these words. Use the plural of each word to complete the crossword puzzle.

Across

1. family

4. baby

5. teddy

Down

1. fairy

2. story

3. puppy

Usually when a word ends with 'f', change the 'f' to 'v' and add 'es' to make it *plural*.

2. Write the plural of each of these words to complete the sentences.

| thie__f__ | hal__f__ | shel__f__ | lea__f__ | wol__f__ |

(a) During autumn, the _____ on our trees turn brown and fall off.

(b) My brother and I went _____ in a new game.

(c) I like to keep the books on my _____ neat.

(d) _____ broke into our home and stole our television.

(e) Mum has lots of pictures of _____ around our house. They are her favourite animal.

Understanding and choosing words

Synonyms

Focus

Synonyms

Definition

- **Synonyms** are words that have the same or similar meaning.

  For example:

  thin – skinny – narrow

  Note: The choice of each synonym depends on the context the word is to be used; e.g. we say a 'narrow' road rather than a 'skinny' road.

Explanation

- Identifying and using different synonyms develops and enriches pupils' vocabulary. Varying vocabulary usage by using appropriate synonyms enhances their written and verbal communication.

Worksheet information:

- As an introduction, show pupils a pair of scissors. Ask them for words to describe the blade. Examples could include 'sharp' or 'pointy', or 'shiny' or 'gleaming'. Explain how these words are similar and are called 'synonyms' and have the same or almost the same meaning.

- Discuss each part of the worksheet with the pupils. They can complete it independently or with teacher assistance as necessary. If they are having difficulty unjumbling the words in Activity 1, give them the first letter of each word as a clue.

- Discuss different synonyms pupils may have chosen for Activity 2 and if all were appropriate for the context in which they were used.

Ideas for further practice

- Pupils brainstorm to list other synonyms for words such as 'big', 'little', 'said' or 'nice'. Discuss appropriate examples of when they would use each synonym and make up sentences to demonstrate this.

- Write the names of pairs of synonyms on blank playing cards, one per card. Pupils can play 'Concentration', finding pairs of matching synonyms. As an extra, pupils must give sentences using each synonym before being allowed to keep matching pairs.

- Solve crossword puzzles as these require pupils to think of synonyms for the answers.

Answers

1. (a) cry – weep
   (b) sick – ill
   (c) stop – finish
   (d) chop – cut
   (e) mend – fix

2. Possible answers:
   soft – gentle, quiet, frail
   walk – hike, trek
   trail – track, path
   easy – simple
   incorrect – wrong
   scared – frightened, afraid
   shout – yell, scream
   cheerful – happy, bright
   nearly – almost, about
   beginning – starting
   worried – upset, concerned
   breaking – snapping
   shouting – yelling, screaming
   swiftly – quickly
   huge – big, large
   grins – smiles

Synonyms

Some words have the same or almost the same meaning.
They are called *synonyms*.

1. Unjumble each word. Draw a line to its synonym.

    (a) yrc _____   • fix

    (b) kics _____   • cut

    (c) pots _____   • weep

    (d) poch _____   • ill

    (e) enmd _____   • finish

2. Write a synonym for each word in brackets.

    'I think we're lost, Sophie!' my older sister, Jacinta, said in a (soft)

    _____ voice.

    We had gone for a (walk) _____ along the forest (trail)

    _____ near our camping spot. We had thought it would

    be (easy) _____ to find our way back by following the

    signs. But we must have taken an (incorrect) _____ turn.

    'I'm so (scared) _____, Jacinta. What do you think we

    should do?' I whispered.

    'Let's go this way and we'll (shout) _____ out now and

    then for help', she said, trying to sound (cheerful) _____.

    After (nearly) _____ half an hour we were (beginning)

    _____ to feel really (worried) _____. Suddenly

    we heard the sound of a branch (breaking) _____

    ahead of us and Dad (shouting) _____ 'Jacinta! Sophie!'

    We hurried (swiftly) _____ towards him with (huge)

    _____ (grins) _____ on our faces!

Understanding and choosing words

Antonyms

Focus:

Antonyms

Definition

Antonyms are words that are opposite in meaning.
Example:

> *quiet – noisy*

Explanation:

- Identifying antonyms develops and enriches pupils' vocabulary and enhances their written and verbal communication.

Worksheet information

- As an introduction, pupils identify 'opposites' in the classroom; e.g. something 'old' and something 'new', something 'shiny' and something 'dull'. Discuss the word 'antonym'.

- Discuss each part of the worksheet with the pupils. Some will be able to complete it independently, others may require assistance.

- Remind pupils of the need to change the boy's name to a girl's.

Ideas for further practice

- Play 'Charades' to guess a word and then say its antonym. The antonym could also be role-played instead of saying it aloud.

- Pairs of pupils make a list of ten words that have antonyms. They write the antonyms for the words in the list on grid paper to make a wordsearch. They swap with other pairs to find the answers.

Answers

1. (a) clean
   (b) night
   (c) unsafe/dangerous
   (d) below

2. *(Girl's name)* woke up *late*. It was Saturday and *she* hoped *she* would be visiting *her* cousins. *She* could tell from the time *she* opened *her* eyes that it was going to be a *cold* day. *Her* room was *dark* and the air felt *cool*. *She slowly* got out of bed and went *downstairs*. *Her mother* and *brother* were looking out the *front* window.

   'Hi *(Girl's name)*', *her mum* said with a *frown* on *her* face. 'Look how *cloudy* and *wet* it is today. It's going to be a *horrible winter's* day. A great day to be *inside*.'

   (Girl's name) was *sad. She wouldn't* see *her* cousins after all

3. Teacher check

Antonyms

Some words are opposite in meaning to others.
They are called **antonyms**.

1. Finish these sentences by writing an antonym for the word in bold print.

   (a) A washing machine makes **dirty** clothes become _____.

   (b) Some animals sleep during the **day** and come out at _____.

   (c) It is **safe** to play in the park but _____ to play on the road.

   (d) The bird flew **above** the water, then dived _____ the surface for a fish.

2. Read the story. Then read it again and write an antonym for each word in bold print neatly above the word.
   Read your new 'opposite' story!

   > **Ethan** woke up **early**. It was Saturday and **he** hoped **he** would be visiting **his** cousins. **He** could tell from the time **he** opened **his** eyes that it was going to be a **hot** day. **His** room was **light** and the air felt **warm**. **He** **quickly** got out of bed and went **upstairs**. **His father** and **sister** were looking out the back window.
   >
   > 'Hi **Ethan**', **his dad** said with a **smile** on **his** face.
   > 'Look how **sunny** and **dry** it is today. It's going to be a **beautiful summer's** day. A great day to be **outside**.'
   > **Ethan** was **happy**. **He would** see **his** cousins after all.

3. Draw a picture of your opposite story.

Understanding and choosing words

Confused words

Focus

quiet/quite, tired/tried, dessert/desert

Explanation

- **quiet/quite**

  Quiet is an adjective that means **still** or **silent**.

  Quite is an adverb. It can mean:
    completely; e.g. *to be **quite** perfect*
    reasonably; e.g. *to be **quite** proficient*.

  The pronunciation of each word is different but if speech is not clear, the difference may not be apparent.

  Confusion occurs in reading and writing as both words contain the same letters with only the last two in reverse position.

- **tired/tried**

  Tired is an adjective that means **sleepy** or **worn out**.

  Tried is the past participle of the verb **to try**, which means to make an effort to achieve something.

  The pronunciation of each word is clearly different. Confusion occurs in reading and writing as both words contain the same letters with only the second and third letters in reverse position.

- **desert/dessert**

  Desert is a homograph and has two different pronunciations and meanings.

  One meaning, which is a noun, is 'a place with little rainfall'. In speech, the emphasis is on the first syllable.

  The other meaning, which is a verb, means 'to run away with no intention to return'. The emphasis is on the second syllable.

  Dessert is a noun which means a 'sweet meal eaten after dinner'. The emphasis is on the second syllable.

  Confusion generally occurs with the spelling. A possible strategy for remembering is that the sweet meal which we often want more of has a double consonant (more), and the desert, which has little rain, has only one consonant (less).

Worksheet information

- Discuss the meaning of each word and highlight the similarities and differences of the spelling of each pair.

- In Question 2, give pupils free rein to explain how they see the similarities and differences of each pair.

Ideas for further practice

- Dictate a short text including all the words. Pupils write the text. Correct as a group/class.

- Make six cards with one of the words written on each card. In small groups, pupils place the cards face down and take turns to choose a card. They explain to the others how the word is pronounced, how it is spelt and what it means.

- In groups, pupils take turns to explain the use of each pair of words.

Answers

1.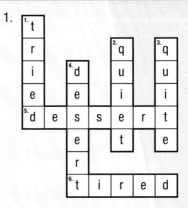

2. Teacher check

Confused words – 1

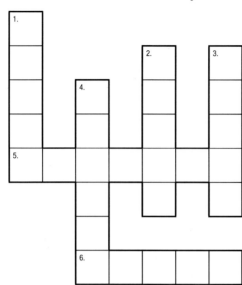

1. Answer the clues to complete the crossword.

Across

5. Eaten after dinner

6. Sleepy

Down

1. Did one's best

2. Without noise

3. 'Yes, you are _____ right.'

4. A place with no rain.

2. With each pair of words, what is the same and what is different?

(a)

quiet and **quite**

(b)

tired and **tried**

(c)

dessert and **desert**

Understanding and choosing words

Confused words

Focus

it's/its

Explanation

- **It's** is derived from the joining of the two words **it** and **is**. As with all contractions, an apostrophe is used to show that a letter has been removed.

  For example:

  > **It's** raining today.
  > **It's** a shame you can't visit.
  > Mum is cross with the puppy because **it's** always chewing our shoes.

- **Its** is not a contraction and therefore does not require an apostrophe. It is a possessive determiner in the same group as **my, your, his, her, our** and **their**.

  For example:

  > The cat licked **its** paws.
  > The dog buried **its** bone.
  > The music lost **its** appeal.

Worksheet information

- Explain how **it's** is derived, what it means and when it is used.
- **It's** can only be used when it is possible to replace it with the words **it** and **is**.
- Show how **its** is a possessive determiner, similar to: e.g. **my** book, **your** ball, **his** bike.
- Give examples of the correct usage of each word for the pupils to understand.
- By knowing how many of each word to write, pupils will be able to check their choices before their work is marked.

Ideas for further practice

- Dictate a short text which includes **it's** and **its**. Pupils write the text. Correct as a group/class.
- On pieces of card, write short cloze texts with **it's** and **its** removed. Pupils place cards with **it's** or **its** written on them, in the appropriate places. Within groups, pupils check each other's work.
- Pupils take turns to explain to each other when each word should be used.

Answers

1. Its	2. Its
3. its	4. it's
5. its	6. Its
7. it's	8. It's

Confused words – 2

It's and *its* have the same sound but they have different meanings.
It's is a contraction and is short for 'it is'.
Its shows ownership.

Read the text and write either *it's* or *its* in each space.
Each time you write a word, draw a tally line in the
table below. Your total should match the totals in the table.

Queen Alexandra's birdwing butterfly

The largest butterfly in the world is the **Queen Alexandra's**

birdwing. 1._____ wingspan can reach up to 30

centimetres.

2._____ natural environment is a small area of rainforest

in Papua New Guinea. This magnificent butterfly does not

have many predators because 3._____ diet when 4._____ a

caterpillar is the leaves of the poisonous pipe vine.

Like all butterflies, 5._____ life begins as an egg, laid only on

the pipe vine. 6._____ life cycle from egg to butterfly takes four

months. A caterpillar hatches from the egg and eats the pipe

vine leaves until 7._____ ready to make a cocoon. 8._____

inside the cocoon that the change to a butterfly takes place.

The Queen Alexandra's birdwing lives for about three months.

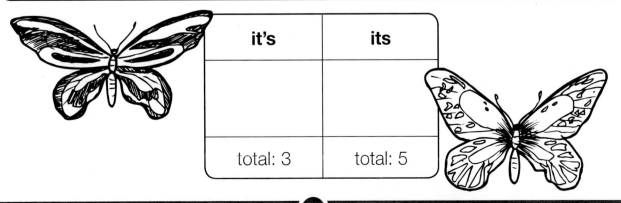

	it's	its
	total: 3	total: 5

Punctuation

Full stops

Focus

Full stops at the end of a sentence

Full stops for abbreviations

Definitions

- **Full stops** are punctuation marks used to show the end of a sentence.

  Example:

  We are going to a special meeting tomorrow.

- An **abbreviation** is a shortened form of a word or phrase. A full stop is used to show that a word has been abbreviated.

  Example:

  Monday – Mon.

Explanation

- Full stops usually show the end of an idea or thought in a sentence. They can also indicate that a break is needed when reading.

- With abbreviations, full stops are not used when the last letter is the last letter of the word being abbreviated.*

  Example:

  street – st, Doctor – Dr

- The necessity for faster communication has contributed to some changes.

  Abbreviations of proper nouns, such as New South Wales (NSW), no longer need full stops. They are now only used to avoid possible confusion.

Worksheet information

- Only abbreviations using full stops are used for this worksheet.

- Read and discuss the information at the top of the worksheet.

- Full stops to indicate the end of a sentence should be added to the text in Question 1.

- Read the instructions for Question 1 (b) and allow the pupils to complete the puzzle independently.

- It is likely that pupils have encountered abbreviations of days and months on calendars. A calendar with abbreviations can be shown to the pupils to assist them to complete Question 2.

Ideas for further practice

- Find and list other abbreviations—those with and without full stops.

- Discuss abbreviations which the pupils may be familiar with relating to SMS messaging.

- Pupils select a portion of text (paragraph) from a library or reading book and count the number of full stops. Hold a competition to see who can find the most full stops in a block of text.

Answers

1. (a) On Friday, 6 December, I finally sent my editor the final pages of my book. I was so relieved to finally be finished! The last few pages of the last chapter took a long time to write, but I was really pleased when they turned out so well. I hope my book sells well, but even if it doesn't, I will be pleased to see it in print.

   (b)

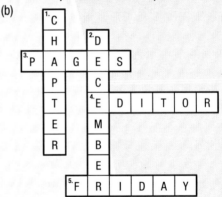

2. (a) Mon.   (b) Tu., Tue. or Tues.
   (c) Wed.   (d) Th., Thu., Thur. or Thurs.
   (e) Sat.   (f) Sun.   (g) Jan.
   (h) Feb.   (i) Mar.   (j) Apr.
   (k) Jun.   (l) Jul.   (m) Aug.
   (n) Sep. or Sept.   (o) Oct.   (p) Nov.

> *Prim-Ed Publishing® employs full stops for abbreviations as recommended by the *Style manual for authors, editors and printers, sixth edition, 2002.*

Full stops

Full stops are used to end a sentence. Full stops can also show that a word has been shortened. These words are called *abbreviations*.

1. (a) Add full stops at the end of the sentences in the text below.

> On Friday, 6 December, I finally sent my editor the final pages of my book I was so relieved to finally be finished The last few pages of the last chapter took a long time to write, but I was really pleased when they turned out so well I hope my book sells well, but even if it doesn't, I will be pleased to see it in print

(b) Find the words in the text which match the abbreviations. Then write the whole word to complete the crossword.

Across	Down
3. pp.	1. ch.
4. ed.	2. Dec.
5. Fri.	

2. Write abbreviations for the words below.

(a) Monday _____ (b) Tuesday _____

(c) Wednesday _____ (d) Thursday _____

(e) Saturday _____ (f) Sunday _____

(g) January _____ (h) February _____

(i) March _____ (j) April _____

(k) June _____ (l) July _____

(m) August _____ (n) September _____

(o) October _____ (p) November _____

Punctuation

Question marks and exclamation marks

Focus

Question marks and exclamation marks

Definitions

- **Question marks** are punctuation marks used to indicate a question.

  Example:

  What are you doing?

- **Exclamation marks** are punctuation marks used at the end of a remark to show strong emotion or feeling.

  Example:

  Stop that! Wow!

Explanation

- A question is an interrogative statement, addressed to someone in order to find out information. When speakers ask a question, their voice is usually raised at the end rather than going down or remaining the same as it does for a sentence. A question mark looks like an upside down hook and is used after a direct question. Questions often begin with words such as **who**, **what**, **when**, **where**, **how** and **why**.

- Exclamation marks usually indicate strong feeling, such as surprise, misery, excitement, disgust, anger or joy. Using an exclamation mark when writing is like raising your voice when speaking. An exclamation mark can be used at the end of an interjection (Oh no!) or a command (Don't touch!) and to add emphasis.

Worksheet information

- Pupils will be familiar with full stops and question marks and would have encountered exclamation marks while reading.

- Read and discuss the explanation about question marks and exclamation marks with the pupils. Give examples of each and find some in shared reading books, then ask the pupils to find others. Emphasise the need for expression to reinforce the fact that exclamation marks are used to indicate strong feelings.

- Explain the instructions for Question 1 and allow pupils to read the text, assisting with unfamiliar vocabulary. Pupils may wish to use different coloured pencils or markers to highlight the question marks and exclamation marks. When highlighting the exclamation marks, ask them to choose a 'strong' colour to represent 'strong feelings'.

- To complete Question 2, pupils may need to quietly say the sentences aloud to determine which ones indicate strong feeling. Ask the pupils to look for clue words, such as 'who', 'what' etc. to help them identify questions. The use of exclamation marks is in some cases subjective, but overuse can reduce their impact.

Ideas for further practice

- Find and read sentences where the 'questioning' word such as 'who', 'does' etc. is not at the beginning of a sentence.

- Make a list of the pupils' favourite exclamations and write them with the exclamation marks in a bold, strong colour.

- Read plays that encourage the expression of strong emotions.

Answers

1. Teacher check

2. (a) exclamation mark, full stop
   (b) full stop
   (c) question mark
   (d) exclamation mark
   (e) question mark
   (f) full stop

Question marks and exclamation marks

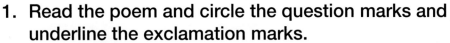

Question marks are used at the end of sentences that ask about things.

Exclamation marks are used at the end of sentences to show strong feelings.

1. Read the poem and circle the question marks and underline the exclamation marks.

Where does the wind come from?

Where does it go when it no longer plays?

Does it fade like the mist on a sunny day

Or fly back to its home?

How cool it must be to soar and glide,

Tossed around without a care!

But sometimes I wish it would just behave

And not mess up my hair!

2. Use the correct mark at the end of each sentence. Choose from a full stop, a question mark and an exclamation mark.

(a) Look ☐ The sailboat is skimming across the lake ☐

(b) The wind is like a naughty child with a bad temper ☐

(c) Why are the leaves being tossed around ☐

(d) Behave yourself ☐

(e) Would you like to be the wind ☐

(f) The wind sometimes makes little whirlwinds ☐

Punctuation
Capital letters

Primary grammar and word study

Focus

Capital letters at the beginning of sentences

Capital letters for proper nouns

Definitions

- **Capital letters** are upper case letters used to begin a sentence, for proper nouns and for titles.

  Example:

  > *My mum's friend came for lunch today.*
  >
  > *Mrs Okley never seems to stop talking.*
  >
  > *The lion, the witch and the wardrobe**

- **Proper nouns** are nouns used to name particular people, places or things.

  Example:

  > *Dr Brooks, London, Mediterranean Sea, Ocean Crescent*

Explanation

- Capital letters are needed for the first word in a sentence. They are larger than most lower case letters.

- Proper nouns can be considered 'special' nouns and so are written with capital letters. Proper nouns include people's names, names of places, days of the week, months, holidays and festivals, countries, nationalities, languages and religions.

Worksheet information

- Give the pupils sufficient time to read through the text. Assist with any words which may be unfamiliar, such as the made-up country names.

- Read and discuss the information about capital letters, including some examples.

- The pupils complete Question 1 independently and Question 2 with a partner.

Ideas for further practice

- The pupils report words relating to Question 2 to the class and collate the information.

- Find capital letters in use in other contexts—book titles, festival names, days of the week etc.

- Ask the pupils to compose a short talk to present to the class which includes as many proper nouns as possible. Other class members, as listeners, tally the number of capital letters in each talk, including capitals at the beginning of a sentence.

Answers

1. (a) Teacher check

   (b) (i) Byzantin, Vekia, Drovia, Thilakus, Newmadia
   - (ii) Byzant
   - (iii) Stripes Street
   - (iv) Lake Beauty
   - (v) Captain Uppercase, Sir Albert Brosk, Dad
   - (vi) January, April, August, November
   - (vii) General Secretary of Defence

   (c) He, His, Last, But

2. Teacher check

> *Prim-Ed Publishing® employs minimal capitalisation for titles of books and other publications as recommended by the *Style manual for authors, editors and printers, sixth edition, 2002.*

Capital letters

1. (a) Read the text.

Captain Uppercase is an officer in the army of the country, Byzantin. He is stationed in the capital city, Byzant, which is a bustling city on the shores of pretty Lake Beauty. He holds a very important position as adviser to Sir Albert Brosk, the General Secretary of Defence. Captain Uppercase advises leaders about defence and safety measures. His job takes him to countries all over the world. Last year, he visited Vekia in January, Drovia in April, Thilakus in August and Newmadia in November. He is well respected around the world, in our country, in our neighbourhood and in Stripes Street. But to me he's just Dad!

Every sentence begins with a *capital letter*. Proper nouns (the names of people, places, days, titles, months and special things) also begin with a capital letter.

(b) Find and write proper nouns from the text.

   (i)   five words which name countries

   _____

   _____

   (ii) the name of a capital city _____

   (iii) the name of a street _____

   (iv) the name of a pretty place _____

   (v) the names of three people _____

   _____

   (vi) the names of four months _____

   _____

   (vii) a title _____

(c) Write four *different* words from the text which begin sentences and are not proper nouns.

   _____

2. With a partner, talk about any familiar proper nouns, such as the names of streets, towns, special places, people, or organisations you belong to.

Punctuation

Commas

Focus

Commas for a series of words, phrases and clauses

Definition

Commas are punctuation marks that can be used to separate words, phrases and clauses to clarify meaning.

Explanation

- In a series, the comma stands for an omitted conjunction, such as 'and' or 'or'.
  Example:

  'I like chocolate, licorice and sherbet' means *'I like chocolate **and** licorice and sherbet.'* The comma has replaced the omitted 'and'.

- Commas can be used for:
  – a series of nouns
  Example:

  The meal consisted of steak, peas and potatoes.

  – a series of verbs
  Example:

  Jason ran, tripped, fell and fainted.

  – a series of adjectives
  Example:

  She was young, beautiful, kind and naive.

  – a series of phrases
  Example:

  He doesn't like washing dishes, ironing clothes or mopping floors.

- A comma placed before the conjunction is called a serial comma and is usually considered unnecessary. The serial comma is necessary if omitting it causes confusion about the meaning of the sentence.
  Example:

  Jason spotted a man running, a girl eating an ice-cream and a fox. **(Incorrect)**

  Without a comma after 'ice-cream', it may seem the girl is eating an ice-cream and a fox!

  Jason spotted a man running, a girl eating an ice-cream, and a fox. **(Correct)**

Worksheet information

- Read the text with the class. Pupils identify the sentences with lists of words and the sentence with the list of clauses.

- Read and discuss the comma rules with the class.

- Pupils determine if the sentences in Question 2 contain a series of words or a series of phrases/clauses before they begin the task. Pupils add the commas where they are needed, following the comma rules.

- Pupils decide if the sentences have been punctuated correctly in Question 3 and rewrite the incorrect sentences in Question 4.

Ideas for further practice

- Pupils write a sentence listing the things they would buy (a series of words) or do (a series of phrases/clauses) if they won the lotto.

- Pupils write a sentence containing a series of phrases/clauses explaining how a clown prepares him/herself for a child's birthday party.

- Pupils explain the comma rules and give examples to pupils from a different class.

Answers

1. Teacher check

2. (a) The weather today is cool, dry and windy.
   (b) We need hammers, nails, glue and a saw.
   (c) Every morning I clean my teeth, wash my face and brush my hair.

3. (a) and (d) incorrect; (b) and (c) correct

4. (a) The monster was huge, green and ugly.
   (d) Jack promised to walk the dog, rake the lawn, wash the car and do his homework.

Commas

> **Commas** are used to separate a list of words or groups of
> words in a sentence to make the meaning clear.

1. (a) Read the text.

> Alex had packed drinks, sandwiches, bubble gum and a radio. Sita brought homemade biscuits, a torch, batteries and playing cards. The children stared excitedly at the tall, mysterious and inviting tree house. It was time to climb the ladder, set up camp, enjoy midnight feasts and tell tall tales.

(b) Circle all the commas and underline the 'and' words used in lists of words and groups of words in the text.

Comma rules
- Put a comma between every word or groups of words in the list except the last two.
- Put '**and**' or '**or**' between the last two items.

2. Add commas where they are needed in the sentences below.

(a) The weather today is cool dry and windy. (1 comma)

(b) We need hammers nails glue and a saw. (2 commas)

(c) Every morning I clean my teeth wash my face and brush my hair. (1 comma)

3. Decide if each sentence is written correctly by placing a 'tick' or 'cross' in each box.

(a) The monster was huge, green, and, ugly. ☐

(b) I collect stamps, coins, shells and badges. ☐

(c) Sarah put on her backpack, opened the gate and ran to the bus stop. ☐

(d) Jack promised to walk the dog rake the lawn wash the car, and do his, homework. ☐

4. There are two incorrect sentences. Rewrite them correctly.

(a) _____

(b) _____

_____

Punctuation

Apostrophes in contractions

Focus

Negative contractions: doesn't, didn't, aren't, isn't, don't, haven't, won't, can't

Definition

- A **contraction** is a shortened word made by joining two or more words and taking out one or more letters. The missing letter or letters is/are replaced by an apostrophe.

Explanation

- Contractions are commonly used in speech and informal writing in English, but infrequently in formal writing.

- When two or more words are joined and contracted, the omitted letter or letters are marked with an apostrophe inserted where the letters were removed. When two words are joined, the spelling of the first word usually remains unchanged.

- The mistake is often made of placing the apostrophe between the two words, such as when using the negative 'not'; e.g. should'nt, do'nt. Pupils will need to be reminded that the apostrophe marks the missing letter, not the space where the two words join.

- Negative contractions can sometimes be written two different ways; e.g. 'You're not going to school', or 'You aren't going to school'.

- Note: There is no contraction joining the words 'am' and 'not'.

Worksheet information

- Read the introduction with the pupils. Discuss how when 'not' and another word are contracted and the other word remains the same, the 'o' is taken out of the 'not' and replaced with an apostrophe.

- Demonstrate circling or erasing the letters that are removed in contractions and replacing them with an apostrophe.

- Pupils will need a number of different coloured pencils or crayons for this activity. They match the contracted word with the two original words, colouring the pair of socks the same colour or with the same pattern.

- With Question 2, pupils write the letter or letters that were omitted to make the contraction.

Ideas for further practice

- At the website <http://www.quia.com/rr/222575.html> is an online interactive game where pupils can practise selecting the separate words that make up certain contractions.

- At <http://www.primarygames.com/contractions/start.htm> is a similar interactive game where pupils decide which contraction is spelled correctly to try and open up a treasure chest.

Answers

1. does not – doesn't; can not – can't;
   do not – don't; will not – won't;
   is not – isn't; did not – didn't;
   have not – haven't; are not – aren't

2. (a) n, o
   (b) o
   (c) o
   (d) o

Apostrophes in contractions

Some words can be joined together to make a new, shorter word. When one or more letters are removed and replaced by an apostrophe, the new, shorter word is called a *contraction*.

When making a contraction with the word 'not', the 'o' is usually removed and replaced with an apostrophe between the 'n' and the 't'. The first word doesn't usually change.
For example:

do + not = don't

There are two exceptions: with 'will not', the spelling changes to 'won't'; and 'can not' contracts to 'can't'.

can + not = can't　　　**will + not = won't**

1. (a) Find a sock with a word that is a contraction of the two words in another sock. Colour the pair of socks the same or with the same pattern.

   (b) Find other pairs and colour them different colours.

2. Write which letter(s) has/have been removed to make each contraction.

   (a) can't　　_____

   (b) doesn't　_____

   (c) didn't　　_____

   (d) aren't　　_____

> **Remember:** In contractions, the *apostrophe* goes where some letters *used to be*.

Punctuation
Apostrophes for possession

Focus

Apostrophes for possession.

Definition

- An **apostrophe of possession** indicates ownership and is placed directly after the owner or owners.

  Example:

  my uncle's cricket bat

  the horses' mouths

Explanation

- To show possession of a noun that does not end in **s**, an apostrophe and the letter **s** can be placed directly after the owner or owners.

  Example:

  the boy's skateboard

  the children's parents

- If a noun ends with an **s** (such as **kids** and **knives**) the apostrophe comes after that **s** and no additional **s** is usually necessary.

  Example:

  the boys' bags

- The possessive pronouns (**ours, yours, theirs, his, hers** and **its**) require no apostrophe and neither does the determiner **its**.

Worksheet information

- Pupils read the introduction. Discuss the position of the apostrophe to indicate ownership; it needs to go straight after the owner and be followed by an **s**.

- Model some examples on the board. Suggest that before using an apostrophe, pupils stop and ask if there is a word in the sentence that denotes something belonging to someone (or something). Write some sentences omitting apostrophes and ask pupils to suggest where the apostrophes should be placed.

- Pupils complete the worksheet. Firstly, they match the items to the characters, using apostrophes of possession. They then choose four things from around the classroom that belong to someone else and list the items, showing ownership. Following this they rewrite each sentence in Question 2, using apostrophes and **s** to show ownership.

Ideas for further practice

- Pupils could design their own superhero at *<http://www.ugo.com/channels/comics/heroMachine2/heromachine2.asp>*, then write a description of him or her using apostrophes of ownership.

  Example:

  'My superhero's cape is red.'

  'The cape's stars are gold.'

Answers

1. (a) the magician's wand
   (b) the queen's crown
   (c) the unicorn's horn
   (d) the giant's club
   (e) the knight's sword
   (f) the dragon's fire

2. (a) Tom's dog is called Bob.
   (b) The camel's hump is huge.
   (c) The cat's tail is long.

Who does it belong to?

To show that something belongs to someone or something, an *apostrophe* and *s* can be added to the end of the word.

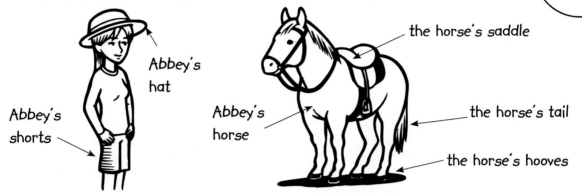

Abbey's hat

Abbey's shorts

Abbey's horse

the horse's saddle

the horse's tail

the horse's hooves

1. Next to each picture, write who owns it and what it is; e.g. fairy's wings.

(a) _____

(b) _____

(c) _____

(d) _____

(e) _____

(f) _____

2. Rewrite these sentences with an apostrophe and 's'.

(a) **The dog owned by Tom** is called Bob. _____

(b) **The hump of the camel** is huge. _____

(c) **The cat has a tail** that is long. _____

Punctuation

Quotation marks

Focus

Quotation marks for direct speech

Definition

- **Quotation marks** are inverted commas used to enclose speech or thoughts.

Explanation

- Quotation marks (also called 'inverted commas' or 'speech marks') are used in writing to show the exact words that someone has said.

  Example:

  'I'm going to the beach', said Teresa.

- Quotation marks are not used for reported or indirect speech, where what was said is reported by a third person.

  Example:

  Teresa said that she was going to the beach.

- Quoted text must start on a new line unless the same speaker is speaking.

  Example:

  'How's your new car?' enquired Tareq.

  'It's fantastic', replied Martina.

- The first word a person speaks begins with a capital letter, even if it begins in the middle of a sentence.

  Example:

  *James shouted, '**Q**uick, hide behind the tree!'*

- A comma usually separates what is being said from the person who is saying it.

  Example:

  *Then Baby Bear said**,** 'Someone's been eating my porridge!'*

- There are differences among British, American and Australian use of quotation marks.

Worksheet information

- Give each pupil a copy of the worksheet and read the introductory text with them. Discuss how in pictures speech is written as a speech bubble, but for writing it is put in quotation marks. Model writing some speech (perhaps a short conversation between two pupils) on the board. Discuss the shape of the quotation marks, which are often like a six and a nine (this is good way for pupils to remember which way to write the quotation marks; six always comes before nine).

- Pupils complete the worksheet by firstly putting quotation marks into the text, then, based on the picture of the alien, writing a conversation using quotation marks.

Ideas for further practice

- In pairs, pupils can write three questions they'd like to ask a third classmate. One pupil acts as an interviewer and ask the questions, while the second pupil writes down exactly what was said in response.

- Pupils could write a script from a short story they enjoy to create a reader's theatre. This is where they read aloud expressively, using their voices, facial expressions and hand gestures to interpret characters in scripts or stories, rather than 'acting'.

Answers

1. They couldn't leave the puppy. It was so cute! 'Can we take it home?' June asked her mum. 'I promise I'll look after it!'
   'He does look like he needs a home', said June's mum, giving it a scratch under the chin.

2. Teacher check.

'Quotation marks', I said.

When we write the words that someone has actually said, we put little marks, called *quotation marks*, around those words.

Quotation marks show where the speaker's words begin and end, and help us to read and understand what we read.

QUOTATION MARKS

Suddenly, Sam pointed to the water.

'Hey, look!' he said excitedly. 'A whale!'

'Where?' Sian asked. 'I can't see it!'

1. Put the quotation marks around the spoken words.

They couldn't leave the puppy. It was so cute!

Can we take it home? June asked her mum. I promise I'll look after it!

He does look like he needs a home, said June's mum, giving it a scratch under the chin.

2. Write what you think is being said in this picture and who is saying it. Use quotation marks.

_____

_____

_____

_____

_____

_____

Figures of speech

Alliteration

Focus

Alliteration

Definition

- **Alliteration** is the repetition of a sound at the beginning of words.

  Example:

  Peter Piper picked a peck of pickled peppers.

Explanation

- Alliteration occurs when the same consonant sound or sound group is repeated at the commencement of two or more stressed syllables of a word group (usually the first sound in a word).
- Activities using alliteration are often used when introducing initial sounds to young pupils.
- Alliteration is often used in nursery rhymes and poetry.

  Example:

  baa, baa black sheep

- Alliteration can make rhymes, poems or songs easier to remember.
- Alliteration is a useful writing tool to create special effects.

Worksheet information

- Allow the pupils to read the text in Question 1, assisting with any unfamiliar vocabulary if necessary.
- Read and discuss the explanation of alliteration, give some examples and ask the pupils to supply some examples as well.
- Using the poem, the pupils circle, count and write the number of alliterative words.
- Question 2 asks the pupils to complete the sentences using the 't' words supplied.

Ideas for further practice

- Identify alliterative words in texts used during shared reading sessions.
- Make up fun tongue twisters to say and illustrate them.
- Find alliterative words in the chorus or verse of popular songs.

Answers

1. (a) Teacher check
   (b) There are 17 words starting with a 't' sound. (Note: 'The' has not been included because it doesn't start with the same sound.)

2. (a) tough   (b) tacos
   (c) tango   (d) track, town
   (e) twelve, toasted

3. Teacher check

Alliteration

1. (a) Read the poem.

> Timothy Tiger was timid and sweet.
>
> Today, he searched for tidbits to eat.
>
> He travelled to and travelled fro
>
> But not a single treat would show.
>
> He tiptoed up and tiptoed down.
>
> He searched up high and searched down low.
>
> Finally, with two tremendous roars,
>
> He took his empty tummy to the takeaway store.

Alliteration occurs when the same sound is repeated at the beginning of words.

   (b) Circle all the words in the poem that begin with a 't' sound.

   How many words did you find? _____

2. **Choose the correct 't' word to complete the sentences. Parts (d) and (e) need two words each.**

tango	tacos	tough	track
town	toasted	twelve	

   (a) Timothy Tiger was not very _____.

   (b) The takeaway store sold _____.

   (c) Timothy loved to dance to a _____.

   (d) The _____ to the shop in _____ was rough.

   (e) Timothy Tiger was so hungry, he ate _____

   _____ sandwiches.

3. **Write a sentence of your own using alliteration.**

   _____

   _____

   _____

Figures of speech

Anagrams and palindromes

Focus

Anagrams and palindromes

Definitions

- An **anagram** is a word made by rearranging the letters of another word.

  Example:

  thorn – north

- A **palindrome** is a word that reads the same forwards and backwards.

  Example:

  eye – eye

Explanation

- Investigating figures of speech such as anagrams and palindromes develops and enriches pupils vocabulary and fosters an interest in language. Working with anagrams, in particular, will help pupils' spelling as they are required to rearrange letters to create new words.

Worksheet information

- To assist pupils in understanding how to create anagrams, make a copy of individual letters of a specific word on separate cards. Pick a word such as 'tub' or 'spot' and ask pupils to rearrange the letters on the cards to make a new word. They can try different combinations until successful. ('Tub' makes 'but' and 'spot' makes 'pots' and 'stop'.)

- When pupils complete Questions 1 and 2, the cards could again be used or they could try writing different combinations on scrap paper. Context clues in the text will also assist.

- The clues, the number of letters in each word and the letters in the box will assist pupils in identifying the palindromes in Question 3.

Ideas for further practice

- Create and distribute sets of word cards that have letters written on them that will make at least two words when the letters are rearranged. Pupils can work in pairs to create anagrams.

- In pairs, pupils create their own palindromes with three letters. Pupils sort through the alphabet using the consonant/vowel/consonant method; e.g. *bab, beb, bib, bob, bub—bib, bob and bub are palindromes.* Dictionaries could be used.

Answers

1. Our family has **two** pets. Whiskers, the cat, is nearly **ten** years old. She still likes to chase mice and **rats**. Last week, she got a **thorn** in her paw. Whiskers **was** very brave when we pulled it out. Toby, our dog, is still a puppy. He loves to chew **shoes** and play tug of war with a **rope**.

2. pets/step/pest

3. (a) mum (b) bib (c) toot (d) pip (e) did

Anagrams and palindromes

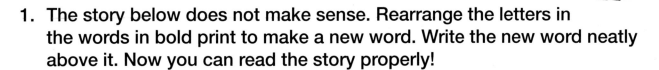

> An **anagram** is a word made by rearranging the letters of another word; for example: *left – felt*.

1. The story below does not make sense. Rearrange the letters in the words in bold print to make a new word. Write the new word neatly above it. Now you can read the story properly!

    Our family has **tow** pets. Whiskers, the cat, is nearly **net** years old. She

    still likes to chase mice and **star**. Last week, she got a **north** in her paw.

    Whiskers **saw** very brave when we pulled it out.

    Toby, our dog, is still a puppy. He loves to chew **hoses** and play tug of

    war with a **pore**.

2. Can you make two different words by rearranging the letters in 'pets'?

    pets _____   _____

> A **palindrome** is a word that reads the same forwards and backwards; for example: *pup – pup*.

3. Use the clues and the letters in the box below to find the palindromes. Cross out each letter as you use it. Each letter can be used only once.

b	t	o	m	i	o
u	b	m	d	p	p
	i	d	i	t	

    (a) Another word for 'mother'. ____ ____ ____

    (b) A baby wears this at meal times. ____ ____ ____

    (c) The sound a car's horn makes. ____ ____ ____ ____

    (d) You will find this inside an apple or a grape. ____ ____ ____

    (e) I ____ ____ ____ not do that!

Figures of speech
Similes

Focus

Similes

Definition

- A **simile** compares one thing with another. Similes are usually introduced by the words 'as' or 'like'.

  Example:

  *He was **as** cunning **as** a fox.*

  *She slept **like** a log.*

Explanation

- Similes are figures of speech. They are examples of figurative language, as opposed to literal language. In figurative language, words are used to create mental images and impressions by comparing ideas. These comparisons help the reader to more clearly imagine the person, place or thing being described.

  Writers use similes to emphasise a certain characteristic. They make writing more interesting, entertaining and colourful, as they often find a link between two unlike subjects.

  For example:

  *'**The children** ran around the playground like a pack of **wild animals**.'*

Worksheet information

- Read the explanation of a simile and discuss the example. Ask the pupils if they can think of any other similes.

- Read the poem with the class. Discuss which word introduces a simile—'as' and 'like'. In Question 1, pupils underline the four similes in the poem and circle the two things being compared in each line.

- Pupils match the nouns that complete the similes in Question 2.

- In Question 3, pupils complete the poem about a monster by choosing nouns to finish each line. Pupils draw their monsters.

- Pupils write a sentence containing the simile stated in Question 4. When completed, ask for volunteers to share their sentences with the class.

Ideas for further practice

- Pupils write a simple simile poem about the beach. Give them a structure to follow.

  Example:

  The sun is as fierce as _____.

  I feel as hot as _____.

  I splash about like a _____.

- In groups, pupils draw around one group member on a large sheet of paper. Pupils write similes about the main body parts inside the outline.

  Example:

  'hair as _____ as _____'

- Work in small groups to think of more similes. Illustrate each one and make a simile book for the reading corner.

Answers

1. (a) and (b) (Note: The words in bold are the things being compared.)

   The beach

   The **sea** is <u>as smooth as</u> **glass**;

   The **sand** on my feet is hot <u>like</u> **fire.**

   The **seagulls** swoop <u>like</u> **vultures**;

   The **sun** is <u>as fierce as an angry</u> **tiger**.

2. (a) as cool as a – cucumber
   (b) as blind as a – bat
   (c) as quick as – lightning
   (d) as light as a – feather
   (e) as warm as – toast

3. Answers will vary

4. Teacher check

Similes

A *simile* compares one thing with another, usually using the words *'as'* or *'like'*; for example:

She slept *like* a log.

The beach

The sea is as smooth as glass;

The sand on my feet is hot like fire.

The seagulls swoop like vultures;

The sun is as fierce as an angry tiger.

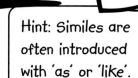

Hint: Similes are often introduced with 'as' or 'like'.

1. (a) Underline the four similes in the poem.

(b) In each line of the poem, circle the two things being compared.

2. Match the beginnings and endings of these well-known similes.

(a) as cool as a   •   • bat

(b) as blind as a   •   • toast

(c) as quick as   •   • feather

(d) as light as a   •   • lightning

(e) as warm as   •   • cucumber

3. Add words to complete this simile poem about a monster. Draw your monster.

The monster is as tall as a _____.

His eyes are black like _____.

His fur is as dirty as _____.

His teeth are sharp like _____.

The monster is as hungry as_____.

And as scary as _____.

4. Write a sentence that uses this simile: *'as flat as a pancake'*.

_____

_____

Figures of speech
Metaphors

Focus

Metaphors

Definition

- A **metaphor** is a comparison between two things without the use of 'as' or 'like'. Metaphors say something *is* something else.
  Example:
    *The **sunset** was a **rainbow of colours**.*

Explanation

- Metaphors are figures of speech. They are an example of figurative language, as opposed to literal language. In figurative language, words are used to create mental images and impressions by comparing ideas. These comparisons help the reader to more clearly imagine the person, place or thing being described.

- Metaphors make writing more interesting, entertaining and colourful. Writers use metaphors to emphasise a certain characteristic of something. A metaphor states that two subjects are the same, which gives one subject the attributes of the other.
  For example:
    *In the playground, the **children** were a pack of **wild animals**.*

  The children have been given the attributes of a 'pack of wild animals' being loud and untamed.

Worksheet information

- Read the explanation of a metaphor and give examples. Ask the pupils if they can think of any other examples of metaphors.

- Read the poem 'The kitten' with the class. Pupils work in pairs or small groups to identify the metaphors in the poem.

- In Question 2, pupils draw lines to match each metaphor with its literal meaning.

- Pupils write a sentence containing the metaphor stated in Question 3. When completed, ask for volunteers to share the sentences with the class.

- Pupils explain and illustrate the metaphors in Question 4.

Ideas for further practice

- Pupils work in small groups to think of common metaphors for people who are: tall, short, silly, angry, beautiful etc.

- Pupils work in pairs to look in familiar texts to locate metaphors.

- Choose one attribute of a monster to write a metaphor about.
  Example:
    hair, fur, eyes, nose, nails, walk, voice
  Collate the metaphors to create a class poem about a monster.

Answers

1. (a) – (b) (Note: The words in bold are the things being compared.)
   The kitten
   The **kitten's claws** are **sharp needles,**
   Her **teeth** are **daggers** and **knives**.
   With **fur** of **soft, white snowflakes**
   And **eyes** two **sparkling bright stars**.

2. (a) sandpaper – rough   (b) blue – sad
   (c) giant – tall   (d) cloud – soft
   (e) bright – smart

3. Answers will vary

4. Possible answers
   (a) cold
   (b) kind

Metaphors

A *metaphor* says one thing is something else.

For example: 'Joey *is* a clown in class'.

The kitten

The kitten's claws are sharp needles,

Her teeth are daggers and knives.

With fur of soft, white snowflakes

And eyes two sparkling bright stars.

1. (a) Read the text and underline the four metaphors.

   (b) In each line of the poem, circle the things being compared.

2. **Match the metaphors in bold with their meaning.**

   (a) Grandpa's hands are **sandpaper**.   •   • tall

   (b) Kiara has been **blue** since Sunday.   •   • soft

   (c) Austin is **a giant**.   •   • rough

   (d) My pillow is **a cloud**.   •   • smart

   (e) David is **bright**.   •   • sad

3. **Write a sentence containing this metaphor: '*a blanket of snow*'.**

   _____

   _____

4. **Explain these metaphors and draw a cartoon for each.**

   (a) **'My feet are blocks of ice'**
   means: 'My feet are very

   _____'.

   (b) **'My gran is an angel'**
   means: 'My Gran is very

   _____'.

Figures of speech

Onomatopoeia

Focus

Onomatopoela

Definition

- **Onomatopoeia** is a word which imitates the sound of what it describes.

  Example:

    plop or **zoom**

Explanation

- Figures of speech are used to make language more interesting, memorable or surprising. There are three distinct groups: phonological figures of speech (based on sound effects); lexical figures of speech (depending for their effect on the use of words); and syntactic figures of speech (depending for their effect on sentence structure).

- Phonological figures of speech include:

  alliteration – the use of the same sound at the beginning of words.

  Example:

    The **s**limy **s**nake **s**ilently **s**lithered.

  assonance – the use of internal rhyme by using the same vowel or consonant sounds within words which follow each other or are close together.

  Example:

    d**ou**ble tr**ou**ble

  onomatopoeia – the use of a word to resemble a sound.

  Example:

    the **babbling** of a stream

Worksheet information

- Read comics available from the library or newsagent or any other texts which use onomatopoeia. Identify and discuss the use of words such as 'POW' and 'Ka-boom!' Ask the pupils why they think the author has used these words in the story.

- Introduce the pupils to the term 'onomatopoeia' and explain that it means a word whose sound reflects its meaning. Use the comics you have read to provide pupils with examples of these types of words.

- Ask pupils to brainstorm and list any words they think are onomatopoeic.

- The worksheet uses the comic format to demonstrate the use of onomatopoeia.

Ideas for further practice

- Pupils may use the word lists developed during the brainstorm to write a simple poem which uses onomatopoeia. Present with appropriate artwork and display.

- Pupils can write and illustrate their own comic strip.

Answers

1. Teacher check

   Words read left to right and top to bottom:

   Kaboom!, Whizzz, THUD!, SPLAT!, Boing!

Onomatopoeia

Onomatopoeia is when a word sounds like what it describes.

1. Read this comic strip. Use the words below to complete the speech bubbles. Draw and write your own ending.

Plop!   *Kaboom!*   *Boing!*   *THUD!*   *Whizzz*   *SPLAT!*

Blast off!

10
9
8
7
6
5
4
3
2
1

The rocket whizzed through space!

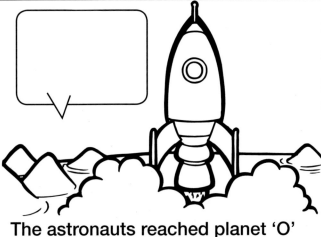

The astronauts reached planet 'O' and landed noisily but safely.

The astronauts stepped off the rocket and landed in mud!

The astronauts heard a strange noise on the other side of the rocks!

Figures of speech
Personification

PERSONIFICATION

Focus

Personification

Definition

- **Personification** is a way of describing non-human things (such as animals and inanimate objects) using human traits and abilities, such as speaking.
  Example:

    *The trees **danced** as the wind **galloped** through the forest.*

Explanation

- Personifying an object or animal can help readers understand, empathise, connect or react emotionally to non-human characters. Personification can inspire imagery and emotion, and provide a different perspective.

- Personification is often used in poetry, fables and fairy tales.

Worksheet information

- Teachers might wish to introduce this worksheet by reading some poetry with personification to the pupils and talking about the human traits or emotions given to inanimate objects or animals. Examples of some appropriate poems include 'Two sunflowers move in the yellow room' by William Blake; and 'In the garden', 'The sky is low' or other poems by Emily Dickinson.

- Introduce the concept of personification by reading the selected poem, fable or story, or by pretending to have a conversation with an every-day object such as a spoon. Explain that, while in real life objects and animals cannot speak or act like people, it is fun and interesting to create stories or poems in which they can.

- Read the worksheet information and discuss the term 'personification' and why it is used in literature. Discuss some of the objects in the classroom and what they might be like if they were imbued with human characteristics: How would the door act? Would it be male or female? How would it feel about being propped open all day and slammed in the wind? Where would it like to go on holiday?

- Pupils choose two classroom objects and give them human emotions and abilities. Pupils may enjoy sharing their 'profiles' with the rest of the class or in small groups.

Ideas for further practice

- The *Narnia* books by CS Lewis contain many animal characters that think, act and have emotions like humans. The pupils might enjoy listening to the books being read to them in parts over a period of weeks and discussing the human characteristics the animals display.

- Pupils could use the concept of personification to write about a topic they are studying. For example, if they are studying water, they could write about the water cycle from the viewpoint of a drop of water.

Answers

Teacher check

Personification

'The sun leans down to whisper that a new day is dawning.
She wakes me with her bright smile, each and every morning.'

In real life, the sun cannot smile or whisper. In stories and poems, we can write about things, like the sun, as if they were people who could do these things and think and feel.

Writing and speaking about animals and objects in this way is called *personification*. It can make stories and poems fun, interesting and imaginative.

Imagine your classroom 'becomes alive' at night. Choose two things in the classroom, draw them as characters and write what they might be like.

Character 1. Name:

Likes:

Dislikes:

Personality:

Character 2. Name:

Likes:

Dislikes:

Personality:
